Indianapolis
a city of immigrants
M. Teresa Baer

INDIANA
HISTORICAL
SOCIETY

www.indianahistory.org | **(317) 232-1882**

Eugene and Marilyn Glick Indiana History Center
450 West Ohio Street, Indianapolis, Indiana 46202-3269

Indiana Historical Society | Indianapolis 2012

This book is a publication of the Indiana Historical Society Press
Eugene and Marilyn Glick Indiana History Center
450 West Ohio Street, Indianapolis, Indiana 46202-3269 USA
http://www.indianahistory.org | Telephone orders 1-800-447-1830
Fax orders 1-317-234-0562 | Online orders @ http://shop.indianahistory.org

The paper in this publication meets the minimum requirements of American
National Standard for Information Sciences—Permanence of Paper for
Printed Library Materials, ANSI Z39.48–1984

Library of Congress Cataloging-in-Publication Data

Baer, M. Teresa, 1956–
Indianapolis : a city of immigrants / M. Teresa Baer.
    p. cm.
Includes bibliographical references and index.
ISBN 978-0-87195-299-8 (pbk. : alk. paper) 1. Immigrants—Indiana—
Indianapolis—History—Juvenile literature. 2. Indianapolis (Ind.)—Ethnic
relations—Juvenile literature. 3. Indianapolis (Ind.)—History—Juvenile
literature. I. Title.

F534.I39A23 2012
977.2'52—dc23

2012003214

THANK YOU TO OUR GENEROUS DONORS

PRESENTING SPONSOR

EFROYMSON FAMILY FUND

A CICF Fund

Inspiring philanthropy

CONTRIBUTING SPONSORS

CICF | The INDIANAPOLIS FOUNDATION LEGACY FUND
CENTRAL INDIANA COMMUNITY FOUNDATION | Inspiring philanthropy

KeyBank

Unlock your possibilities

morales group

Gerald and Dorit Paul

The Reuben Family Foundation, Inc.

USAFunds

WITH ADDITIONAL SUPPORT FROM

ICEMILLER LLP
LEGAL COUNSEL

THE INDIANAPOLIS STAR

La Plaza
· Serving · Educating · Celebrating · Connecting

Printing PARTNERS

EDITORS' NOTE

The political boundaries of nations are ever changing. For the purposes of this booklet, written for high school students and a general audience, we have chosen the most current maps to depict national and regional boundaries. It is for this reason, for example, that Turkey appears on both the European and Middle Eastern maps. In a similar vein, ethnic designations change from time to time. The editors of this booklet have used 2000 and 2010 U.S. census headings as a guide for the various ethnic groups. Although this may cause concern, this rather arbitrary decision was made because even individuals within a particular group often disagree upon designations for their group in both the historical record and in today's media.

To Jim Wills for ongoing support;
and to past and present members of the Indiana Historical Society Press and
the Indiana University–Purdue University, Indianapolis School of Liberal Arts
for their gifts of education and mentoring.

Acknowledgments

The author is grateful for the assistance of the following individuals: Sergio Aguilera; The Efroymson Family Fund, a fund of the CICF; Elaine Rosa, Indiana Historical Society, for consultation on the development of the booklet; Wendy L. Adams and Karen M. Wood, freelance editors, and Lois Allis, IHS Press intern for research assistance; Ray E. Boomhower and Kathleen M. Breen, IHS Press editors.

The author would also like to thank the scholars who reviewed a draft of this booklet:

Robert G. Barrows, Indiana University–Purdue University, Indianapolis
Nancy Conner, Indiana Humanities Council
John A. Herbst, Indiana Historical Society
Wilma L. Moore, Indiana Historical Society
Elaine Rosa, Indiana Historical Society

May Lin Russell of Indianapolis performs the "Seaside Girls" dance at the second annual Asian Festival presented by the Asian American Alliance and Indy Parks and Recreation at Garfield Park, May 2009.

Participants in the Summer Discovery Program at La Plaza in Indianapolis.

Contents

Indianapolis: A City of Immigrants is available for purchase or as a free pdf download at **shop.indianahistory.org/indyimmigration**

Indianapolis: A City of Immigrants Teacher's Guide is available as a free pdf download at **http://www.indianahistory.org/immigrationguide**

The First Hoosiers
Native Americans and Europeans

Everyone on earth comes from somewhere. But the ancestors of most people did not originate in the country where their descendants live today. They moved here from elsewhere.

Biologists and other scientists along with archaeologists and other social historians have tracked the first human beings to Ethiopia in Africa. From there they spread around the globe over millions of years.

Naturally, people moved to places close to Africa first—Asia and Europe—and eventually they made their way to the Americas. The first people who came to America were later called "Indians" by Christopher Columbus. Scientists and social historians believe they came from Asia. Because they were here first, the ones who came after them—from Europe, Africa, the Middle East, and new Asians—called them natives. Today, these first peoples living within the United States are known as Native Americans.

Native Americans were the first people to settle in the land we know as "Indiana"—which means the land of Indians. The stories of the different tribes of these people are much the same as the stories of people everywhere: A group of people lives in an area where there is sufficient food to eat, where the weather is temperate enough to survive, and where there are materials to shelter them from cold, rain, and heat.

When a group of people, such as a tribe, grows too large to live in an area—when food or water grows scarce, when the weather becomes too difficult for too long, or when predators (either animals or other tribes) are threatening to extinguish them—then part or all of the tribe packs up and moves away (migrates) to a new place that will sustain them. Sometimes they fight battles to win land settled by others.

Such movements of tribes occurred in and around Indiana before and after Europeans came. Indians fought each other and different groups of Europeans in the age of the French fur trader (1534–1763)

and in the days of British colonial America (1763–76). By the American Revolution (1776–83) when the first people known as Americans came to Indiana, there were several tribes here—the Miami, Potawatomi, Wea, Shawnee, and a few others. Most lived along the Wabash River, but some, such as the Delaware, lived along portions of the White River, near the present-day Marion–Hamilton County line, and in northern Morgan County.

Native Americans sustained themselves by growing food, gathering herbs, nuts, berries, mushrooms, roots, and other forest life, and by hunting. This was their economy. They added to their economy by trading first with the Europeans and then with the Americans. The French had come to America primarily seeking both a trade in the

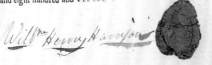

Artist George Winter lived in Indiana from 1837 to 1844 and captured scenes of Native Americans in Logansport and elsewhere in the state. Here he depicts an encampment of Indians in the Indiana wilderness.

fur of animals abundant to North America, such as beavers, and also seeking converts to the Roman Catholic faith. Fur traders were stationed in what became Montreal, Quebec, but they also traveled with, lived among, and intermarried with natives. A few French people were among the first whites to settle in Indiana, near present-day Fort Wayne, Lafayette, and Vincennes. Their descendants, families of mixed French and native heritage, helped Americans led by George Rogers Clark capture Vincennes from the British during the American Revolution.

BY WILLIAM HENRY HARRISON,

GOVERNOR OF THE INDIANA TERRITORY, AND SUPERINTENDANT OF INDIAN AFFAIRS.

Whereas *Benoist Besayon* of the county of *Knox* hath made application for permission to trade with the *Miamis* nation of Indians, and hath given bond according to law, for the due observance of all the laws and regulations for the government of the trade with Indians that now are, or hereafter may be enacted and established, licence is hereby granted to the said *Benoist Besayon* to trade with the said *Miamis* nation, at their town on the *Wabash* and there to sell, barter and exchange with the individuals of the said nation, all manner of goods, wares and merchandizes, conformably to the laws and regulations aforesaid; but under this express condition and restriction, that the said *Benoist Besayon* shall not, by *his* servants, agents or factors, carry or cause to be carried to the hunting camps of the Indians of said nation, any species of goods or merchandize, and more especially spirituous liquors of any kind ; nor shall barter or exchange the same, or any of them, in any quantity whatever, on pain of forfeiture of this licence, and of the goods, wares and merchandize, and of the spirituous liquors which may have been carried to the said camps, contrary to the true intent and meaning hereof, and of having *his* bond put in suit: and the Indians of the said nation are at full liberty to seize and confiscate the said liquors so carried, and the owner or owners shall have no claim for the same, either upon the said nation, or any individual thereof, nor upon the United States.

This licence to continue in force for one year, unless sooner revoked.

GIVEN under my hand and seal, the *Thirtieth* day of *December*, in the year of our Lord one thousand eight hundred and *Seven*.

Willm Henry Harrison

By this 1807 license William Henry Harrison, governor of the Indiana Territory, permitted Benoit Besayon of Knox County to trade with the Miami Indians on the Wabash River. Trading with Native Americans was one of the ways Americans began to develop an economy in Indiana. Indians would sell pelts they harvested from beaver, deer, and other animals to American fur traders for money. The traders would sell the natives items such as tools, weapons, and cookware. In turn, American fur traders auctioned off pelts to companies to make clothing, blankets, and other items.

In this painting artist Frederick C. Yohn shows the victory of George Rogers Clark and the French and Indian townspeople of Vincennes over British forces in 1779, during the American Revolution. The townspeople helped win back their town and the fort and became loyal citizens of the fledgling United States.

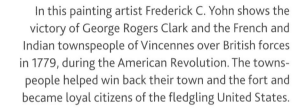

Not long after winning independence from Great Britain, Americans began coming to Indiana in droves, moving the Indians onto bits of land called reservations and eventually pushing most of them out of the state. The Delaware in central Indiana agreed to move west according to the 1818 Saint Mary's (Ohio) treaty, also signed by the Miami. However, some Native Americans along the Wabash River stayed by becoming landowners and others returned from exile. Such large numbers were here by the mid- and late nineteenth century that Indiana had two tribes, the Potawatomi along the Michigan-Indiana border, and the Miami Tribe of Indiana, along the Wabash River in north-central Indiana.

Americans quickly became the majority of people in the state. Many Americans did not like the Indians because they lived differently than Americans.

A painting of Chief Francis Godfroy, of French and Miami heritage, in 1827 at the Treaty of Fort Wayne, Indiana, by artist James Otto Lewis.

Indians lived communally, sharing their land among all their people rather than owning individual plots. Individual natives raised crops or hunted or gathered food or made clothing for all the people in their community—not just for their own family. Even though Indians joined Christian churches, they kept their ancient spiritual beliefs.

Americans, especially those who had just won a war to free themselves from the British king and to create a democracy, believed in individual freedom. They were excited to have the opportunity to support their families by themselves and wanted to be independent, own land individually, and build personal wealth. They also wanted to build a prosperous economy with roads, schools, businesses, and thriving towns. Consequently, Indians either kept to themselves on the land they owned or they tried to blend into the American culture. Often, they kept their ethnicity a secret in order to be accepted, and some were thought of as blacks.

After enduring a century on reservations or in hiding, many Native Americans served during World War II. Afterward, large proportions of Native Americans moved to urban areas to attend college or work in the era's booming factories. By 2000 more than 39,000 Native Americans from more than 150 tribes lived in Indiana. Today, more of these Native Americans call Marion County home than any other Indiana county— enriching Indianapolis's economy as well as its culture.

Native Americans from many tribes gather each year for a powwow at the Eiteljorg Museum in Indianapolis.

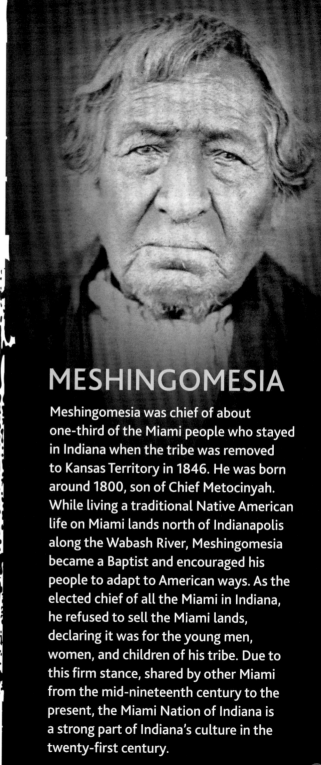

MESHINGOMESIA

Meshingomesia was chief of about one-third of the Miami people who stayed in Indiana when the tribe was removed to Kansas Territory in 1846. He was born around 1800, son of Chief Metocinyah. While living a traditional Native American life on Miami lands north of Indianapolis along the Wabash River, Meshingomesia became a Baptist and encouraged his people to adapt to American ways. As the elected chief of all the Miami in Indiana, he refused to sell the Miami lands, declaring it was for the young men, women, and children of his tribe. Due to this firm stance, shared by other Miami from the mid-nineteenth century to the present, the Miami Nation of Indiana is a strong part of Indiana's culture in the twenty-first century.

Indianapolis Beginnings
American Settlers from the British Isles

Before a treaty with the Delaware signed away the area where Indianapolis now sits, Americans began migrating here. They had originally moved into southern Indiana from the northern tier of southern states, for example, Virginia and North Carolina, or from eastern states, particularly Pennsylvania. Their parents and often their grandparents had lived in colonial America, arriving from northwestern Europe—England, Wales, Scotland, northeastern Ireland, Germany, and France. The reasons they left their native countries fall into a handful of categories called "push factors." Most immigrants left to escape war, famine, religious persecution, a lack of good farm land, or other economic reasons.

Once the British colonies became well established, northwestern Europeans came for a variety of "pull factors," which were incentives to immigrate to America. They came to join family members or neighbors. Those with money intended to better themselves through owning and cultivating land. The less-fortunate immigrants sought to learn a trade or to work, save money, and purchase land. They tended to live within communities that shared their country of origin, language, and religion. They desired to become self-sufficient farmers and perhaps own businesses.

As land on the East Coast became more crowded, the colonists moved west and south to the natural

This drawing depicts Washington Street in the village of Indianapolis in 1825. Settlers were just starting to clear the forest and build what would become the state capital. Washington Street became part of the National Road in 1829, expanding east and west across the middle of the state and connecting the East and West Coasts of the United States.

Amos McCormick came to Indianapolis as an infant in fall 1820. His father, Samuel, and Samuel's brothers, John and James, and their families were among the earliest settlers in the new capital. Descendants of early Irish immigrants to the British North American colonies, the McCormick families traveled from Pennsylvania to Ohio and then to Indiana. In this 1909 photograph Amos is sitting at the table that the Indiana state commissioners used when they were selecting the site for the city. Samuel's family moved to Hendricks County in 1836.

barrier formed by the Appalachian Mountains, which run from Canada to Alabama. After the Revolutionary War, Americans broke across the Appalachians, moving west from Pennsylvania or north and west from new states such as Tennessee and Kentucky. Their journeys were a continuation of their families' quests for self-sufficiency and the right to live according to their chosen values rather than by a state's values.

The two groups of Americans, from the East and the upland South, continued moving into the Old Northwest Territory (which became the states of Ohio, Indiana, Illinois, Michigan, Wisconsin, and part of northeastern Minnesota) as the Treaty of Saint Mary's (1818) opened up the center of Indiana for settlement. Indiana legislators, working in the state's first capital, Corydon, determined to establish a new state capital in central Indiana. Commissioners led by John Tipton selected "the east bank of the White River at the mouth of Fall Creek" for a town to be called Indianapolis. The community was laid out or "platted" in 1821.

The first American settlers who came to Indianapolis from the East and the South had disagreements. In general, easterners, especially members of the Friends or Quaker churches, opposed slavery, while southerners were in favor of it or neutral about it. In time, easterners such as Calvin Fletcher and Caleb Mills advocated the establishment of public schools, whereas many southerners were wary about government involvement in education.

This photo of Aletha Coffin at her flax wheel was published in a 1908 yearbook for the Western Yearly Meeting of Friends (Quaker) Church in Plainfield, Indiana. A widow from North Carolina, Coffin joined the Mill Creek Meeting house near Amo, Hendricks County, Indiana, in 1853. Quakers from North Carolina had been settling the area since 1820.

The Irish Come to Indianapolis

Indianapolis's growth was initially hindered by its lack of natural transportation routes. The White River was too shallow for boats much of the year, and there were no roads. So, it was quite a boon to Indianapolis when Indiana began constructing a canal system in the 1830s. The Central Canal in Marion County was completed in 1836, although it was never connected to the state's other canals. Two years later the National Road (US 40, which originally ran east to west from Atlantic City, New Jersey, to San Francisco, California) was completed through the young town.

The canal and roads brought new businesses and people to Indianapolis—new American settlers and foreign workers, especially Irish and Germans, who were building the transportation systems. The Irish arriving in the nineteenth century were a different group than earlier Scots-Irish immigrants, Protestants whose families had immigrated to America from northeastern Ireland and whose ancestors had originated in Scotland. The Irish who worked on the canals and roads were primarily Catholic. They had come to escape the massive industrial development of their country, a process that was pushing them off their traditional farms and depriving them of a means to earn a living.

Recruiters looking for canal workers traveled to New York and Pennsylvania offering wages of $10 per month. They enticed thousands to come and build Indiana's canals, primarily the very poor Irish immigrants, who arrived daily in eastern harbors. Other new Irish and German immigrants signed up to help build the National Road across Indiana. Not only did Indianapolis

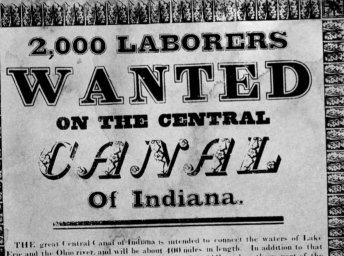

This map created in 1939 by Harry O. Garman shows both built and proposed canals in Indiana during the nineteenth century. As the map shows, Central Canal was finished only from Broad Ripple to Bluffs (now Waverly), Indiana.

have a major canal and highway by 1840, but it also had new groups of foreign residents, Irish and Germans in particular.

A potato famine in Ireland, as well as the building of railroads across Indiana from the 1840s through the Civil War (1861–65), brought many more poor

This advertisement from 1837 attempts to lure workers to build Indiana's Central Canal by offering $20 per month, food, lodging, and the availability of cheap land for farming. The thousands of Irish and Germans who helped build Indiana's transportation routes—canals, roads, and railroads—vastly increased Indiana's ability to attract businesses and develop its economy.

Irish Catholics to Indianapolis. Irish immigrants had a difficult life in Indianapolis at first. Contemporary accounts relate that Americans disliked their Catholic religion and were initially horrified by canal and road crews' shantytowns, drunkenness, public fighting, and poverty. Over time, however, the Irish in Indianapolis settled into lives with stable working conditions. They raised and educated their families and participated in church and community activities. The Irish tended to settle on what became the near west side of town in Saint Anthony and Saint John Parishes and on the near south side in areas that would be known as Irish Hill and Fountain Square. In addition to working in construction and on railroad jobs, Irishmen also worked in the Kingan meatpacking company, which began recruiting workers in Ireland in 1862, or as policeman or firemen. Many Irish women worked as domestic servants in wealthy private Indianapolis homes.

The History of the Catholic Church in Indiana by Charles Blanchard contains numerous biographical sketches of Irish Catholic immigrants who settled in Indiana. Among these are sketches for several individuals named Carr. Martin Carr, who was born in County Galway, Ireland, in 1851, immigrated to Indianapolis in 1871, and first worked for the railroads. Within a few years, he was working as a stable hand at Kingan and Company, where he was in charge of two horses. Eventually, the company owned sixty horses, and Martin was foreman of twelve stable men. He married Kate McCarty, whose father, Lawrence McCarty, was from Ireland.

Martin and Kate had three children and were members of Saint Bridget Parish.

Another sketch describes the life of John E. Carr, who was born in Kenosha, Wisconsin, in 1863. John's parents were both from Ireland, his father, Manies Carr, from County Donegal and his mother, Mary (Laughlin) Carr, from Dublin. Manies was a tanner and currier. After living in Wisconsin, the family moved to Indianapolis in 1881, where Manies died two years later. One of John's brothers died in a railroad accident, one sister married and moved to Missouri, another married and stayed in Indianapolis, and an unmarried brother also resided in Indiana's capital. For more than twelve years John worked in the boiler shops of the Big Four Railroad Company in Brightwood, a neighborhood on Indianapolis's east side. Then he began working in the insurance industry, first as a solicitor, working his way up to assistant manager within four years. John married Maggie Monaghan, daughter of Timothy and Ellen Monaghan, both natives of Ireland, in Indianapolis in 1892. However, Maggie died five years later. Along with many other Irish, John was a member of Saint Patrick Parish.

Blanchard also relates a brief history of the Patrick and Ellen (Cook) Carroll family of Kilarney, County Kerry, Ireland, through their son Thomas P. Carroll, who was born in 1871 and came to Indianapolis in 1892. Thomas had four brothers and two sisters.

A member of the Richens Timm Academy of Irish Dance performs for a crowd at the Indianapolis Irish Fest, 2004.

Samuel Kingan brought his meatpacking plant from northern Ireland to Indianapolis in 1862, where it continued in business until 1966. The Irish made up a large portion of Kingan's workforce.

His mother and three brothers stayed in Ireland; his father, one brother, and two sisters immigrated to America. Of those who immigrated, one sister lived in Ohio with her husband. Another sister, Kate, worked as a housekeeper for Patrick, John, and Thomas. John became a member of the fire department, and Thomas worked at the Vandalia freight depot, then at Kingan's until 1898. After that time, he worked for the Big Four Freight Depot. Thomas was a member of Saint John Catholic Church in downtown Indianapolis.

The children and grandchildren of Irish immigrants thrived in Indianapolis for the most part. The city came to accept the Irish because they improved its economy and increasingly blended into mainstream American society. Today, the Indianapolis community savors the annual celebrations of Saint Patrick's Day and Irish Fest, as well as Irish music, food, and beer year-round.

Indiana's Capital Grows
Germans Call Indianapolis Home

By the American Civil War, there were more than 1,700 individuals in Marion County who had been born in Ireland, representing around 26 percent of the county's foreign-born population. As large as this group was, however, German immigrants were present in even greater numbers. Nearly 4,000 German-born people lived in Marion County according to the 1860 federal census, constituting nearly 60 percent of the county's foreign-born population.

Of Indianapolis's 18,611 residents in 1860, less than one-third were born outside the country. In Marion County as a whole, the countries from which immigrants came other than the German states and Ireland included: England (359 residents), France (211), Scotland (185), Switzerland (88), Canada (84), Italy (19), Wales (18), Holland (13), and a smattering of other European countries. Only nine immigrants were non-European; one was African. In addition, there were 825 African Americans.

One of every five people in the Indianapolis area in 1860 came from a German-speaking region, in Europe. This included present-day Germany and areas in: Austria, Hungary, Russia, Bohemia, Romania, Switzerland, Liechtenstein, Italy, Alsace, Lorraine, and Luxembourg, where pockets of people were of German ethnic origin. Germany itself was not a single nation but more than thirty small kingdoms, duchies, principalities, and city states.

German-speaking people came to the United States during the British colonization era and were among the earliest Americans in the Old Northwest. Many German Americans fought alongside George Rogers Clark during the Revolutionary War and William Henry Harrison during the War of 1812. German-speaking Moravian missionaries lived among and taught Christianity to the central Indiana Delaware in the 1790s. German religious leader Johann Georg Rapp brought a group of utopian Christian followers to New Harmony, Indiana Territory, in 1814.

Published in 1833, this German immigration guide introduced the United States to Germans. It described the country's religion, politics, society, and included reports on German settlements.

After 1815 German immigration increased dramatically. Germans left a Europe that had tasted a republican government through the revolutionary efforts of Napoleon Bonaparte, who ultimately was defeated. Many Germans—Protestants, Catholics, and Jews—preferred American democracy over the kings and princes that were regaining power, and they disliked the compulsory military conscription policies of those rulers.

The economy was also a factor. Europe was experiencing poor harvests at a time of overpopulation. Meanwhile, industrialization in England was undermining traditional cottage industries on the continent. For example, machine-woven cloth costs much less money to produce than traditional hand-woven cloth. England was producing large quantities of such products and selling them cheaply, while other Europeans, including Germans, were producing far fewer products on their home-based looms at higher costs. They could not compete with English industries. Then, when industrialization did come to the German states, such improvements as mechanical looms not only put home weavers out of work but they also required a smaller workforce, leaving many without a livelihood.

In addition to the attractions of a republican form of government and abundant economic opportunity, German families living in the United States wrote to relatives and friends in the "old countries," encouraging them to come to America. These words of encouragement, multiplied many times over in letters and German-language newspapers, resulted in Germans pouring into America through the mid-nineteenth century. Many German-speaking families brought money to buy land in southern and central Indiana, where they settled as farmers prior to the Civil War.

Many poor Germans worked alongside the Irish on Indiana's canals, roads, and railroads, following the travel routes they were building

A factory produces items of clothing faster and cheaper than one or two seamstresses making clothing in their homes. This photo is of Kahn's Tailoring Factory in Indianapolis in 1907. The factory employed many Jewish immigrants.

Workers for the Guedelhoefer Wagon Company in front of the store, circa 1915. In 1873 German immigrant John Guedelhoefer founded a wagon company that specialized in making delivery wagons for ice, dairy, and bakery products. The company remained in the Guedelhoefer family for a century. Pictured here are Harry Guedelhoefer, in straw hat; John Guedelhoefer, to left of car; and August Guedelhoefer (owner of company) to right of car.

into Indianapolis and settling there. Indianapolis Germans added greatly to the city's economy by specializing in a variety of occupations: they were carpenters, shoemakers, tailors, coopers, blacksmiths, grocers, and merchants. They settled just northeast of the capitol and on the south side of town, where they built Christian churches and Jewish meeting houses and clustered in the neighborhoods around them.

A separate wave of Germans began arriving in 1848 and after, fleeing a failed revolution in the German states. They were middle-class intellectuals who moved to American cities such as Indianapolis, Cincinnati, and Milwaukee. They became influential politically, promoting the abolition of slavery, equal rights for women, and education as the basis of progress, and opposing temperance movements. The "Forty-Eighters" believed in reason rather than religion and socialism rather than capitalism. They established clubs, called "vereins" to foster personal fitness, the arts, mutual aid, and politics.

This petition for naturalization for Friedrick Buesking from 1921 states that Buesking was born in Menden, Germany, in 1854 and his wife, Ellen, was born near Menden. At the time of this petition, they had three children and were farmers in Cumberland, Indiana, just east of Indianapolis.

In the latter part of the nineteenth century, Indianapolis's German American immigrants established more than fifty vereins. For example, in 1867 Indianapolis German immigrant farmers on the city's south side formed the Gardeners Benefit Society of Indianapolis to promote farming while keeping within the highest possible standards. Many of the members established greenhouses and truck gardens, providing year-round vegetables to the city's markets. To join, one had to be between twenty-one and fifty years of age and physically healthy. Members received health and death benefits, and the society also loaned money to help new immigrant members.

German immigration increased after the Civil War through the 1880s, mostly from the eastern German states. Indianapolis's German Americans were involved in politics, education, and the arts. They published several German-language newspapers and opened numerous parochial and secular schools where German was taught. Through the efforts of Indianapolis school board members such as Clemens Vonnegut, German Americans introduced physical education and manual technical training into the city's public school system, creating the nation's oldest school of physical education (now part of Indiana University in Indianapolis) and also in Manual Training High School, which opened in 1894.

A native of Muenster, Westphalia, Vonnegut (1824–1906) came to Indiana in 1851 after traveling to New York City on business. He opened a general merchandise store with partner and former schoolmate Charles Volmer. Vonnegut took sole control of the business in 1858, changing it to a hardware store. The Vonnegut Hardware Company did business in downtown Indianapolis for more than a hundred years.

The Vonnegut Hardware Company on Washington Street in Indianapolis, 1878. Founded by Clemens Vonnegut in 1858, the company remained in the Vonnegut family until 1965.

Vonnegut became well known for his civic leadership. In 1851 he, along with several of Indianapolis's German leaders, formed the Indianapolis Turner Society (*Turngemeinde* or *Turnvein*), a venue for German immigrants to discuss liberal political and social views, and a platform from which to promote German language, culture, and physical education. In 1859 Vonnegut assisted in establishing Indianapolis's German-English Independent School, which taught lessons in both German and English. He also supported an 1869 law authorizing the teaching of German in public schools.

A supporter of free thought—a humanist, antireligious, proscience movement among German immigrants—Vonnegut became a prominent member in Indianapolis's Free-Thinkers Society during the 1870s and 1880s. In 1889 he published a free-thought tract, *A Proposed Guide for Instruction in Morals.*

Vonnegut married German immigrant Catharine Blank in 1853, and they had four sons: Clemens Jr. (1853–1921), Bernard (1855–1908), Franklin (1856–1952), and George (1860–1952). His great-grandson, Kurt Vonnegut Jr. (1922–2007), was a notable author of American counterculture novels.

The Germans in Indianapolis suffered discrimination from nativistic Americans who loathed

Members of the German Gardeners Benefit Society, a group centered on Indianapolis's south side, at a picnic in German Park in 1911.

languages other than English, religions other than Protestantism, and political views other than their own. Beer-drinking Germans and Irish were reviled especially after they gained their citizenship and loudly proclaimed anti-temperance opinions. During World War I hysteria against Germans became the American norm, as America joined the British and French against Germany and its allies. In a backlash against German culture Indiana schools were banned from teaching the German language. Anti-Germanism did not last through the Great Depression or World War II, however, as Americans of German heritage made a conscious decision to make their ethnic background secondary to their loyalty to the United States.

The Northern City of Indianapolis
An African American Journey

Newly arrived Irish and German immigrants suffered discrimination and endured occasional acts of hatred from Americans who feared immigrants would take their jobs or influence their society with strange customs. Later generations, however, increasingly blended into mainstream society. In contrast, Indiana's African Americans and their descendants suffered racial discrimination for nearly two centuries.

The first African Americans in Indiana were enslaved by French people, living mostly around Vincennes. Although the Northwest Ordinance of 1787 and the Indiana Constitution of 1816 forbade slavery, it existed in Indiana. If slave owners emancipated their slaves, the practice often continued under the cloak of indentured servitude. Some early recorded blacks in Indianapolis were servants of two city planners. One servant, Cheney Lively, became a property owner.

Prior to the Civil War blacks could not vote, serve on juries or in the militia, testify in court against whites, and there were no provisions for black children to receive a public education. An 1831 Indiana law required blacks entering the state to post a $500 bond. Many blacks indentured themselves to raise the money. The 1830 federal census highlights this reality: of twenty-one households in the capital containing blacks, only five were headed by blacks—Lively and four men, two of whom became victims of hate crimes. In 1838 an angry white mob attacked the family of James Overall, and in 1845 John Tucker was murdered by drunken white men in downtown Indianapolis. Article XIII of Indiana's revised 1851 constitution barred blacks from entering the state.

Perhaps because of the antiblack environment, Indianapolis's pre-Civil War, African American population was never more than 5 percent. By 1840 only 195 blacks lived in Indianapolis, most working at manual labor or as domestic servants in white households. They started black churches, such as Bethel African Methodist Episcopal Church (1836) and the Second Baptist Church (1846). As with other immigrant communities, the churches provided help to the needy, schools for children, and safe places to discuss political and social issues. Indianapolis blacks also started mutual-aid societies and fraternal organizations, such as the Mason's Union Lodge Number 1, begun in 1842.

The pre-Civil War decades were filled with increasing tension between whites and blacks in Indianapolis, reflecting the growing American national agitation over slavery. Factions such as the Quakers and German abolitionists opposed nativists who wanted to rid the city of blacks and foreigners. Meanwhile, the city's African Americans gathered in conventions to discuss ways to improve their people's conditions, to fight colonization societies that wanted to send them to Africa, and to use political means to gain citizenship rights.

The Civil War brought many changes. A large percentage of Indiana's African Americans enrolled in the Twenty-eighth Regiment of U.S. Colored Troops. Blacks from the upper South fled north in droves, more than doubling Indiana's black population by 1870. More blacks came to Indianapolis than anywhere else in the state. By 1900 blacks comprised nearly 10 percent of the city's population.

The Civil War also changed federal and state laws. By 1870 black men had voting rights and could sit on juries. Nonetheless, from the 1860s through the 1960s, African Americans in Indianapolis as elsewhere struggled against discrimination in education, employment, housing, and public accommodations. African Americans countered discrimination by working through mutual-aid organizations and taking political action. One Indianapolis resident who helped start a mutual aid society was former slave Eliza Goff, who was born in North Carolina during the 1820s and moved to Indianapolis before 1870. A widow, Goff was concerned about elderly ex-slaves. Along with other black Indianapolis women, she founded the Alpha Home Association in 1883, a nursing home for elderly and infirm African Americans. Goff worked as a maid for Pauline Merritt, who donated the land and house for the home, which opened in July 1886. Goff served as president for one year and died in Indianapolis in 1898.

Indianapolis's African Americans built their community in a variety of ways, simultaneously helping to add to the city's economy. Black teachers and ministers operated all-black schools and served as community leaders, helping to create a black middle class. The few blacks able to obtain higher education began entering professions such as law, medicine, and business. Along Indiana Avenue, just northwest of the city's center, restaurants, saloons, groceries, barbershops, dentists, blacksmiths, caterers, clubs, and other black businesses developed. African American newspapers such as the *Indianapolis Recorder* gave a voice to the community, and individuals such as Lillian Thomas Fox (1866–1917) also wrote about the black community in white newspapers.

Meanwhile, blacks were voting Republican, the party of Abraham Lincoln. By 1880 the first black Hoosier was elected to a state political office—Indianapolis's James Hinton was elected to the Indiana General Assembly. Three other African Americans succeeded him, including Indianapolis schoolteacher Gabriel Jones.

Map of African Nations, circa 2003.

During World War I, African Americans began a "great migration," which was the movement of people from the rural South to cities in the North. In 1910, 89 percent of blacks lived in the South, nearly three-fourths of them in rural areas. By 1970 half of African Americans lived in the North, most in cities. Indianapolis's population was more than 12 percent African American by 1930. Blacks fled the South following an insect infestation, which devastated cotton crops, looking for better opportunities in war-created jobs and hoping to escape racial segregation. Most Indianapolis migrants were disappointed; only menial jobs were available to blacks and after the war discrimination did not subside. The Ku Klux Klan, which supported native-born, white, Protestant Americans, achieved statewide power in the 1920s.

One of the hundreds of African Americans who came to central Indiana in the 1920s was Harvey N. Middleton (1895–1978), an African American doctor born into a South Carolina farm family. At the age of ten, Middleton watched as his mother lay seriously ill and a white doctor did nothing to help her. With his parents' encouragement, he decided to become a doctor. He graduated from Benedict College in Columbia, South Carolina, in 1919, went to Boston University for three years, and received his medical degree at Meharry Medical College in Nashville, Tennessee, in 1926.

In 1928 Middleton came to Anderson, Indiana, joining the staff at Saint Joseph Hospital. He moved to Indianapolis in 1936 and wanted to practice medicine at Indianapolis's City Hospital (later Wishard Memorial and now Sidney and Lois Eskenazi Hospital), but due to segregation practices he could only volunteer in the outpatient clinic. During this time, he started a private practice, giving electrocardiograms on a cardiette machine he had purchased. From the late 1920s through 1940s Middleton completed postgraduate studies in heart disease at Harvard Medical School, the University of Michigan, and the University of London, England. He later joined the staffs of: Indianapolis City, Saint Vincent, Methodist, Community, and Winona Hospitals.

Church supper at the Bethel African Methodist Episcopal Church in downtown Indianapolis, circa 1960.

January 14th 1809

This day John Smith and a Negro Man named Jacob Ferrel, aged about Thirty four Years, and lately held by said John Smith in the State of ~~Virginia~~ North Carolina as a Slave came before me Clement Nance Clerk pro Tem. of the Court of Common pleas of the County of Harrison, and it is agreed by and between the said John Smith and the said Jacob Ferrel negro that he the said Jacob Ferrel is to serve the said John Smith his Heirs &c from the date hereof untill the 14th day of of January One thousand Eight hundred and Twenty two and as a compensation for such services the said John Smith engages to give unto the said Jacob Ferrel on demand one grey mare four Years old named Tib, and a red Cow with a white face, As prescribed by a law of this

Some southern slaveholders who immigrated to Indiana brought their slaves and signed them into indentured servitude, according to territorial laws. This 1809 document from Harrison County, Indiana, states that Jacob Ferrel, a slave from North Carolina, would receive a horse, a cow, and his freedom in exchange for serving thirteen years as an indentured servant for the family that had previously owned him.

Middleton became a civic leader, helping to establish the Morgan Health Center adjacent to Flanner House, an African American social-service agency on Indianapolis's near north side. He cochaired the state campaign for the United Negro College Fund in the early 1950s and served on the Young Men's Christian Association's board.

As Middleton was becoming established in Indianapolis, World War II erupted, breaking down barriers for African Americans who flocked into military service and into the cities for jobs. President Franklin D. Roosevelt's administration enforced equity in hiring practices for government-contracted work, and Indiana governor Henry F. Schricker's administration encouraged employment of black workers. Black migration increased again and remained steady the rest of the century. By 1990 blacks comprised more than 20 percent of Indianapolis's residents.

At the end of World War II, African Americans renewed their fight

Indianapolis Recorder offices, circa 1907. This newspaper began operation on Indiana Avenue around 1900 with a focus on African Americans in local communities. Black-owned businesses, such as the *Recorder*, helped expand Indianapolis's downtown economy. After 1920, many blacks also worked in the city's industrial sector, providing labor that was crucial for economic growth.

against discriminatory practices, aided by organizations such as the National Association for the Advancement of Colored People, which had many white members as well as black. As a result, in Indiana a 1949 law barred segregated schools; laws in 1961 and 1963 outlawed discrimination in access to jobs and in public places such as restaurants, and in 1965 a Fair Housing Law passed. Backing these up was the federal Civil Rights Act of 1964. After struggling against prejudicial laws, African American Hoosiers were finally on legal footing with all other Americans—whether native- or foreign-born.

African American World War I soldier, Les Brown, from Indianapolis, circa 1917.

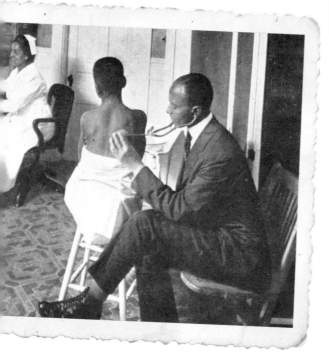

Doctor Henry Lytle Hummons with his nurse and two young patients at an Indianapolis clinic, 1919.

As of 2010 nearly 30,000 people had emigrated from the African continent to central Indiana. Representing about 3.3 percent of Marion County's population, they include people from 150 cultures and 7 language groups. War refugees, students, and professionals are among these African immigrants. Many study to become American citizens, such as Kidist Harting from Ethiopia, shown here at her citizenship ceremony in November 2010 with members of the Indianapolis chapter of the Sons of the American Revolution, Stuart Hart (left) and Ron Darrah (right), who helped officiate at the ceremony.

Indianapolis as Refuge
Eastern and Southern Europeans Flock to the City

Pre-World War I Immigration

The prejudice that African Americans suffered in the early twentieth century was shared by new immigrants from southern and eastern Europe, most impoverished Jews or Catholics. New waves of immigration sprang from political turmoil roiling in lands between western Europe and Russia and in the Balkan region. These immigrants were peasants from tiny villages and farms within huge empires. "Nationalist" forces were striving to consolidate places with similar backgrounds and cultures, breaking up the empires and creating struggles that neither concerned nor helped the peasants.

In Russia new laws freed peasants from serfdom to large landholders, but mechanizing agriculture was pushing thousands of laborers off farms at the same time that anti-Jewish laws in Russian lands were displacing Jews. In wave after wave, southern and eastern Europeans came to America. By the turn of the twentieth century their different languages, religions, and cultures evoked fear, anger, and violent acts in the nativist population, and they became targets of the Ku Klux Klan in the 1920s.

Although eastern and southern European immigrants came from places we know today as Italy, Greece, Hungary, Poland, and Russia, grouping them within nations they never knew seems ironic.

Having been separated for generations, various townspeople spoke a language in different dialects, wore different clothing, cherished different memories, practiced religion in different ways, told different stories, and played different music. To an outsider, they seemed similar, but to people from different villages, they were not.

In Indiana the majority of these immigrants added substantially to the state's economy by working in the toughest jobs—coal mining near Terre Haute, in Lake County's steel mills, and extracting natural gas and oil in north-central Indiana. Similar to the early Irish, they lived in crowded temporary shacks

Celebration of Greek Independence Day by the Greek School students of Indianapolis, April 1939.

and earned little money (much of which they sent home). Most eastern Europeans were young males, trying to save money to purchase land back home and become farmers. Many left, only to return, some again and again. Unable to start a new life in their homeland but with few connections to Americans, they huddled in their close-knit communities, single men in boardinghouses, several families living in a house, surrounded by people from their home villages.

Few southern and eastern Europeans came to Indianapolis before 1900. In 1910 there were 663 Italians, 290 Greeks, 861 Hungarians, and 1,260 people identified as "Russian," who were of various origins, mostly Slavic, and about 80 percent Jewish. These immigrants helped grow the city's economy in a variety of ways. Besides working at railroad jobs, Indianapolis's Italian immigrants peddled fruits and vegetables. Greeks opened dry cleaners, restaurants, florists, bakeries, and taverns. Hungarians worked in slaughterhouses, meat-packing companies, and at Malleable Castings Company. Eastern European Jews worked in garment and shoe manufacturing, as bakers, and sold fruit and sundries in stalls outside the City Market.

In Indianapolis, Holy Rosary Catholic Church was started for Italians on the southeast end of downtown. Greeks established

Map of the European nations, circa 2003.

Holy Trinity Greek Orthodox Church in a rented room on South Meridian Street, living around Military Park and east around Highland Park. Hungarians settled in Haughville on the near west side of Indianapolis. The majority were Roman Catholic, although some joined Hungarian Reformed and American Presbyterian churches, and many were Jewish.

Jewish people had come to America throughout the nineteenth century, and founded the Indianapolis Hebrew Congregation in 1856. Isolated from these "American Jews" in numerous ways, newly arrived eastern European Jews lived, worked, and conducted religious services alongside their fellow eastern Europeans, such as a south-side neighborhood where Jews organized a synagogue in 1870 and purchased a building on South Meridian in 1882.

Because census takers a century ago tended to count immigrants as part of national groups, some ethnic groups, such as Slovenes, were lost in the early counts. Originally from the Balkan area adjoining Italy and the Germanic states, Slovenes began coming to Indiana in response to recruitment from the states' mines and mills. The majority settled in Haughville, on the west side of Indianapolis, and worked at Malleable Castings Company. They established Holy Trinity Roman Catholic Church and school and the Slovenian National Home for recreational activities. By 1920 approximately 1,200 Slovenes lived in Indianapolis.

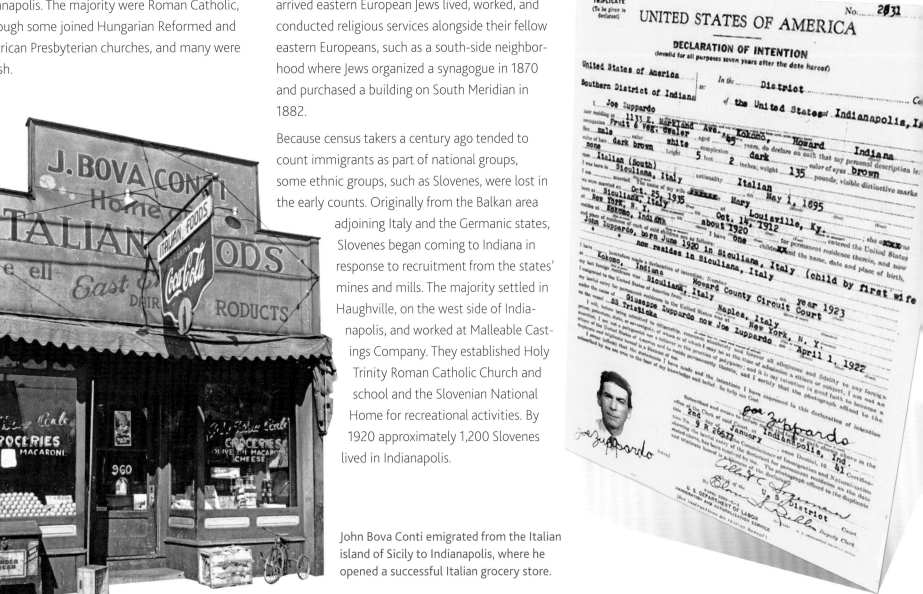

Citizenship document of Giuseppe (Joe) Zuppardo, recorded in Indianapolis in January 1941. Zuppardo immigrated to the United States in 1922 from southern Italy.

John Bova Conti emigrated from the Italian island of Sicily to Indianapolis, where he opened a successful Italian grocery store.

One Slovenian was Joseph S. Zore (ca. 1871–1929), who immigrated to the United States in 1892 from what was then Austria. On August 29, 1902, Zore married Victoria Sebanc, who had emigrated from what would become the capital city of Slovenia, Ljubljana. Sebanc, a maid who could read and write, had arrived at Ellis Island, New York City, twenty days before she and Zore were married. For much of his life, Zore worked for an Indianapolis foundry as a patternmaker. He became a U.S. citizen in 1906 in Marion County. In the 1920s he owned and operated a soft drink saloon at his residence in Haughville. Joseph and Victoria had eight children: Joseph A. (born 1904), John (born 1905), Victor (born 1908), Victoria (born 1910), Ludmilla (born 1912), Ferdinand (born 1914), Louis (born 1919), and Paulina (born 1921).

Another Haughville Slovenian was Ignaz Turk (1881–1928), originally from Bucka, a small town southeast of Ljubljana. Turk immigrated to the United States in September 1900 aboard *La Touraine*. On the ship's manifest, Turk stated he was a tailor, but by 1910 his occupation was molder at a Haughville foundry. In July 1902 Turk married Mary Pushner (1883–1962) in Indianapolis. Mary was from Srednje Gorica, in what is currently Italy. She had also immigrated in 1900. Ignaz and Mary had five children: Frank (1903–1986), John (1904–1927), Louise (1908–1998), Mary (1908–2000), and Leona (1914–1981).

Top: Mary Pushner Turk with her twin girls (right) Mary and (left) Louise, ca. 1909.

Above: The Joseph S. Zore family, circa 1920s. Clockwise from center, Seated: Joseph S., Louis, Victoria, Paulina (Polly). Back Row, left to right: Ludmilla (Millie), Ferdinand (Fred), Joseph A., Victor, John, and Victoria

Right: The Zore and Turk families were united on June 16, 1926, when Joseph A. Zore married Louise Turk (one of the twins).

A U.S. Law Curtails Immigration

As thousands of southern and eastern Europeans poured into America, many Americans became increasingly unhappy, complaining that immigrants took American jobs, sent the money home, spoke unintelligible languages, and isolated themselves in impoverished neighborhoods. Public pressure resulted in a 1924 federal law severely curtailing the annual number of immigrants entering the United States. Until 1965, when the law was changed, immigration quotas were kept very low.

The two world wars and the cold war between the democratic West, headed by America and western Europe, and communist countries, headed by the Soviet Union and China, affected the types of individuals who came to Indiana. The 1940 census shows immigrants in Marion County from Bulgaria, Czechoslovakia, Latvia, Lithuania, Romania, and Yugoslavia, as well as the places mentioned above, and the 1980 census also shows the Soviet Union. Many were political refugees fleeing Nazi Germany or the communism of the Soviet Union. Many immigrants were highly educated and had held positions in government, universities, and big business. After World War II, individuals who had lived in refugee camps came to the United States as "Displaced Persons." When the Soviet Union, in rare moments, lifted its ban on migration, those who left were also considered Displaced Persons. Around 200,000 Hungarians, known as "Freedom Fighters,"

who had revolted against their communist government, fled to the United States soon after a revolt failed in 1956.

Eastern and southern Europeans arriving in the mid-1950s joined the children and grandchildren of the earlier immigration waves. These later immigrants tended to live as individuals rather than in ethnic pockets and they assimilated more quickly into American culture. Nevertheless, the descendants of the earlier groups have combined with the later arrivals to reinvigorate and celebrate their common heritage and identity through ethnic festivals, clubs and associations, food, dress, stories, and music.

Mr. and Mrs. Berek Kaplan arrived in Indianapolis in March 1949 as Jewish refugees displaced by World War II. They are shown here at the Hotel Michigan with their two children, Rosza, age three, and Moszesz, age two.

The Circle City Thaws
Asians Migrate Slowly but Steadily to Indianapolis

Chinese and Japanese Hoosiers

Change is the key to understanding immigration during the last decades of the nineteenth century and the first half of the twentieth century. As in Europe, empires were crumbling in Asia during this period. Asians had long traded with the West, supplying tea, spices, and other commodities. Western governments wanted to increase profits by controlling the trade, and so they forced the ancient, self-contained regimes of China and Japan into trade agreements. Stresses from this fundamental change—to realize that other people besides themselves were powerful and to step outside of their traditional ways of interacting—eventually led to the transformation of cultures thousands of years old.

As their country opened to outside influence, many Chinese were recruited to help build the vast railway systems across the American West. However, Americans did not want them to stay. Their hairstyles, clothes, language, and Confucian values were totally unfamiliar to Americans. Fear and prejudice, along with political disputes between the American and Chinese governments, led to the Chinese Exclusion Act of 1882, denying immigration and citizenship rights for most Chinese. The 1924 Oriental Exclusion Act barred immigration and naturalization for all Asians.

From 1943 through 1965, U.S. immigration laws relaxed slowly, eventually permitting an annual quota of Asians into the country and allowing them to become citizens. As a result of the exclusion laws, Indiana was home to only a handful of Chinese and Japanese prior to 1900. Most of the Chinese lived in Indianapolis, along Fort Wayne and Massachusetts Avenues, where they ran laundries, restaurants, and social clubs. The 1910 census showed 273 Chinese in the state.

Exemptions to the immigration laws during some periods allowed students, teachers, merchants, government officials, ministers, newspaper editors, and tourists to come to the United States. Thus, Chinese who came from the 1880s through 1950 were students attending American colleges and people from China's elite classes. One of these was Alfred Tsang, who was born in New York, but lived in China from age three through fourteen. His father was a treaty

U.S. Army Air Corps airman Alfred Tsang, age twenty-one, during World War II. Tsang was born in New York, but raised in China until age fourteen. He and his family came to Indiana after he retired from the U.S. Air Force. Tsang earned a law degree from Indiana University and worked as an Indiana deputy attorney general until retiring. He pursued civic and volunteer work and several writing projects before his death in 2010.

merchant who was denied U.S. citizenship under the exclusion laws. Nevertheless, he permitted Tsang to join the U.S. Army Air Corps during World War II. After the war, Tsang finished his education and became an engineer, moving to Indianapolis in 1967. He and his wife raised three children. Tsang was one of the founders of the Indianapolis Association of Chinese Americans in 1973. At age forty-five he returned to school to study law and was the deputy state attorney general in the 1980s.

Only a handful of Japanese came to Indiana before 1945. After Japan bombed Pearl Harbor in 1941, the U.S. government relocated more than 110,000 Japanese Americans from the West Coast to guarded internment camps. Meanwhile, during World War II, 33,000 Japanese Americans fought in the U.S. military or served as interpreters or doctors, and some attended college.

Earlham College in Richmond, Indiana, and the Disciples of Christ, headquartered in Indianapolis, helped bring many former Japanese internees to Indiana. By 1960 more than 1,000 Japanese Americans lived in the state, including war brides of American soldiers and Japanese professionals.

Map of the Asian nations, circa 2003.

MONGOLIA

NORTH KOREA

JAPAN

SOUTH KOREA

KYRGYZSTAN

TAJIKISTAN

CHINA

TAIWAN

NEPAL

BHUTAN

BANGLADESH

MYANMAR [FORMERLY BURMA]

LAOS

PHILIPPINES

THAILAND

VIETNAM

CAMBODIA

BRUNEI

MALAYSIA

MALAYSIA

INDONESIA

SINGAPORE

INDONESIA

EAST TIMOR

George and Jean (Kanno) Umemura are typical of Japanese Americans who moved to Indianapolis. Their families were relocated to Idaho's Minidoka camp from Seattle, Washington. George, Jean, and her sister attended different midwestern universities. After being released from the internment camp, Jean's parents moved to Michigan, where Jean and George were married. The couple and their children moved to Indianapolis when Eli Lilly and Company recruited George, and Jean taught school for thirty years. They helped found the Hoosier Chapter of the Japanese American Citizens League, George serving as its first president in 1976.

Korean, Vietnamese, and Southeast Asian Hoosiers

In 1980 Indiana was home to around 8,000 Chinese and Japanese Americans and more than 7,000 individuals from Korea, Vietnam, Laos, and Cambodia. The immigration of Koreans and Southeast Asians to the United States was due generally to the cold war and particularly to the Korean War (1950–53), and the Vietnam War (1950–75). Korean college students, orphans adopted by Americans, and wives of U.S. servicemen began arriving in the United States in the 1950s.

Indiana's colleges attracted hundreds of Korean students, many of whom became doctors, engineers,

Chinese American Bobby Fong leans against a statue of the school's bulldog mascot during a tour of the Butler University campus shortly before he became its president in 2001. He served in this capacity until 2011.

Manager Nopihisa Iwamoto of the Sakura Japanese Restaurant, Indianapolis, cuts a piece of tuna as he prepares to make some sushi, circa 2007.

and scientists. By the 1970s there were approximately 800 Korean Americans in Indianapolis. Many of them were Protestants due to the missionary work of Methodists and Presbyterians. They established an interfaith church, which split years later into several denominations, including Catholic and Baptist. They also started a Korean Language School for adopted children and their parents and other Korean Americans.

Two Koreans who came to America as students were Han Won Paik and his wife Chinok Chang Paik, who settled in Indianapolis in 1962. Both enjoyed careers at Indiana University–Purdue University, Indianapolis—Han was a physics professor and Chinok taught math and statistics. They raised three children, and Chinok later worked as an actuary at an Indianapolis insurance company.

Following the Vietnam War, America began accepting refugees from communist regimes in Vietnam, Laos, and Cambodia. Waves of refugees arrived after 1975. During the late 1980s, this immigration included increasing numbers of nonrefugee immigrants. By 1990 there were almost 3,500 Southeast Asian immigrants in Indiana. Of these, 600 Vietnamese, 76 Laotians, and 106 Cambodians lived in Marion County.

While most Vietnamese refugees could read and write, less than half from the other areas were

Jason Nguyen, a graduate student in ethnomusicology at Indiana University, Bloomington, plays a Vietnamese monochord Dan Bau at the second annual Asian Festival presented by the Asian American Alliance and Indy Parks and Recreation at Garfield Park in 2009.

literate. A 1983 national study of the jobs where Southeast Asian refugees were working reflects their range of educational levels—from professional/technical to farmers/fishers. The religious beliefs of Southeast Asians are predominantly Buddhist, with strong influences from Catholicism, Hinduism, and animism, a belief in spirits of natural things and creatures.

Seventeen-year-old Laung Khan Kho Khai at Chin National Day festivities in 2010 in Indianapolis. He and his family are Burmese (present-day Myanmar) refugees who fled their country due to its current military government. According to various sources, between 5,000 and 8,000 Burmese refugees lived in the central Indiana area in 2010, many of them in the Southport/ Perry Meridian and North Central school areas.

Filipino Hoosiers

The Philippine Islands were a U.S. colony from 1898 until 1946, when they achieved full independence. Therefore, few Filipinos immigrated to Indiana until after World War II. A few college students were attending Purdue and Indiana Universities as early as 1904. Filipinos who had served in the U.S. armed forces during World War II and their families settled here after 1945. The largest group of Filipinos, English-speaking professionals and their families, came after 1965, when national quotas ended and preference was given to individuals with skills considered important to the United States. This group has contributed greatly to the field of medicine. Filipinos have made important contributions to the Indianapolis community. Two examples are Maria Lagadon, a Spanish teacher in the Indianapolis Public Schools, who founded the Barangay (social) Club of Indianapolis for Filipinos in 1960; and Rolando A. DeCastro of the Indiana University School of Dentistry, who was also a medical illustrator and artist and the coeditor of a textbook on oral surgery. Filipinos also own hundreds of small businesses in Indiana. The 1990 census showed a Filipino population of nearly 5,000, dispersed throughout the state, with the largest concentrations in Marion and Lake Counties.

The U.S. Census of 2010 indicates a large population of Asian Americans in Indiana—nearly 704,000. The numbers with Chinese ancestry tripled since 1990; and those with Philippine and Korean ancestry nearly doubled. Indianapolis had more than 17,000 Asian American residents in 2010, most from China, the Philippines, Korea, Vietnam, and Japan, in that order.

In the twenty-first century, Indiana's civic, business, and educational leaders enjoy strong partnerships with their counterparts in Asian countries. These partnerships draw students, professionals, and big business into the state, bringing both jobs and annual revenue. In 2007 Asian-owned businesses in Indiana (including Asian Indians) employed nearly 25,000 people and earned sales of $3.4 billion.

Wili de la Rosa in 2010. De la Rosa immigrated to Indianapolis from the Philippines in 2007 with his wife, Melinda, and their three youngest children, joining family in the area. Since then he has volunteered in many capacities, most notably helping immigrant refugees from Burma, Africa, and Iraq. The refugees grow crops as part of a farm program created by a partnership among the Refugee Resource and Research Institute of Indianapolis, local churches, and Waterman's Farm Market. The refugees keep half the produce and donate the other half to a local food bank.

New Faces in Indianapolis
Middle Easterners and Asian Indians at the Crossroads

Middle Easterners

Prior to World War I, the Ottoman Empire, which had reigned over the Balkans, most of southwest Asia, the north African coast, and what is now Turkey since the mid-1500s, was crumbling. While eastern Europeans fled to America in droves when the Austrian–Hungarian and Russian Empires were disintegrating, relatively few Middle Easterners came to the United States. It may be because most Ottoman people were Muslim and America was primarily Christian and Jewish. Nearly all of the Middle Easterners who immigrated before the 1920s were Christians from the areas known today as Lebanon, Syria, and Egypt.

When the Ottoman Empire was strong, its armies protected its Christian minorities, who were important for European trade. As the empire weakened, the Christians feared for their safety. Having long been in contact with American missionaries, many decided to move to the United States. Most early Middle Eastern immigrants belonged to religions associated with the Roman Catholic and Greek Orthodox Churches, the Coptic (Egyptian Christian) Church, or were Protestant or Jewish.

By 1890 only 216 Hoosiers claimed Middle Eastern ancestry. Initially employed as peddlers or factory or farm workers, they saved money to start small businesses. Many moved to Indianapolis, near the state's transportation and industrial center. In the 1890s Francis Riszk and Najeeb and David Kafoure were peddlers in the capital city. David and Saada Kafoure opened a dry-goods store, which thrived for fifty years. Nick Shaheen's Oriental Rug Emporium and Dayan's Linen Store, owned by a Jewish Syrian, also conducted business in downtown Indianapolis.

In the 1920s, there were more than 3,500 Middle Easterners in Indiana. Indianapolis Syrians mainly lived on the city's east and southeast sides, where they inaugurated a social club and built Saint George Orthodox Church.

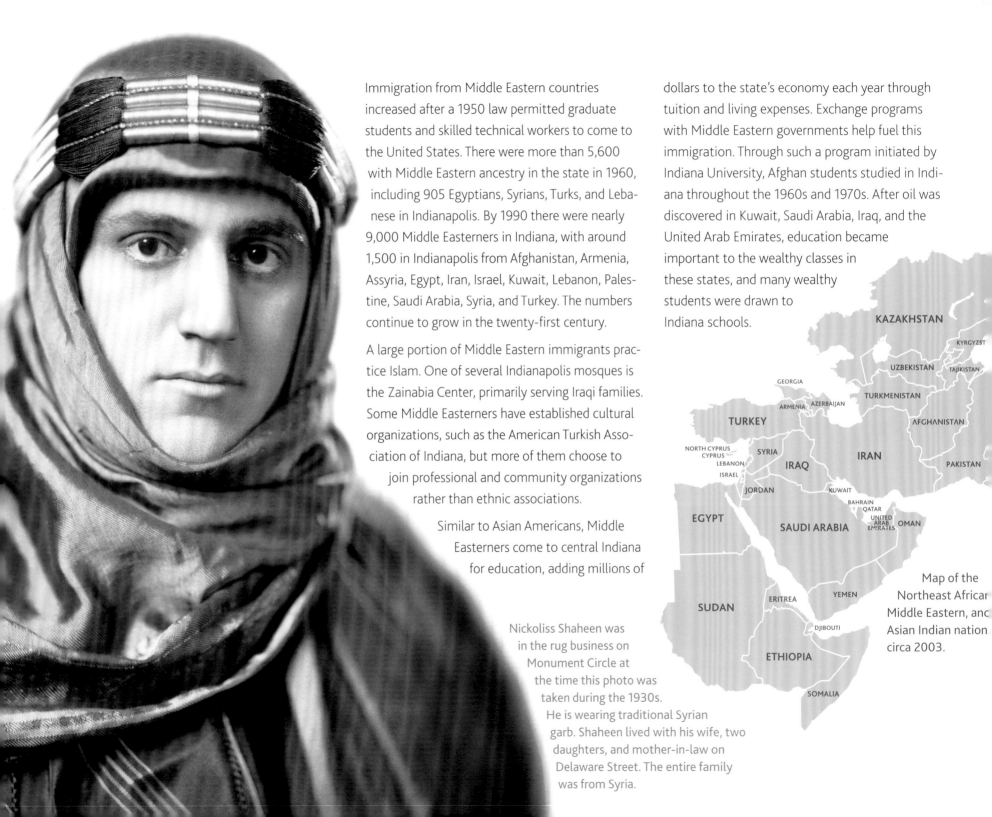

Immigration from Middle Eastern countries increased after a 1950 law permitted graduate students and skilled technical workers to come to the United States. There were more than 5,600 with Middle Eastern ancestry in the state in 1960, including 905 Egyptians, Syrians, Turks, and Lebanese in Indianapolis. By 1990 there were nearly 9,000 Middle Easterners in Indiana, with around 1,500 in Indianapolis from Afghanistan, Armenia, Assyria, Egypt, Iran, Israel, Kuwait, Lebanon, Palestine, Saudi Arabia, Syria, and Turkey. The numbers continue to grow in the twenty-first century.

A large portion of Middle Eastern immigrants practice Islam. One of several Indianapolis mosques is the Zainabia Center, primarily serving Iraqi families. Some Middle Easterners have established cultural organizations, such as the American Turkish Association of Indiana, but more of them choose to join professional and community organizations rather than ethnic associations.

Similar to Asian Americans, Middle Easterners come to central Indiana for education, adding millions of dollars to the state's economy each year through tuition and living expenses. Exchange programs with Middle Eastern governments help fuel this immigration. Through such a program initiated by Indiana University, Afghan students studied in Indiana throughout the 1960s and 1970s. After oil was discovered in Kuwait, Saudi Arabia, Iraq, and the United Arab Emirates, education became important to the wealthy classes in these states, and many wealthy students were drawn to Indiana schools.

Map of the Northeast African, Middle Eastern, and Asian Indian nations circa 2003.

Nickoliss Shaheen was in the rug business on Monument Circle at the time this photo was taken during the 1930s. He is wearing traditional Syrian garb. Shaheen lived with his wife, two daughters, and mother-in-law on Delaware Street. The entire family was from Syria.

Egyptian American Amani Qulali opened the Cairo Café on Lafayette Road at the end of 2005. She is holding a plate of koshory, a traditional Egyptian dish.

Immigrants from the Middle East work as scientists, professors, engineers, doctors, and business people. For example, a Kurdish Syrian immigrant, Mazen Ayoubi, is founder and president of Architecture International Consulting, with an office on the far north side of Indianapolis. Ayoubi is also a founding member of the Interfaith Alliance of Indianapolis and serves on the Board of Trustees of HelpLead.org, an organization focused on building schools and learning centers in impoverished areas around the world to promote self-reliance and economic stability in partnership with local communities.

Salwa Zenhom is an Egyptian-born Muslim who grew up in Indianapolis. When this picture was taken in 2001 she was a student at Indiana University–Purdue University, Indianapolis.

Asian Indians

Asian Indians come from countries that lie between today's Middle East and Asia, including India, Bangladesh, Pakistan, Nepal, Bhutan, Tibet, and Sri Lanka. Similar to their neighbors, most immigrants from the Asian Indian region came to the United States after 1960. Although less than 500 Asian Indians called Indiana home in 1960, there were nearly 17,000 living in the state by 2004. More than 3,000 Asian Indians were living in the capital city in 2009.

Asian Indians began coming to the United States when the immigration laws were changed to favor highly educated individuals. Thus, Asian Indians can be found in Indiana's universities and in the fields of medicine, engineering, and science. The 2000 census showed that a great majority of Asian Indian Hoosiers had earned at least a bachelor's degree.

There are also many business people among Indianapolis's Asian Indians. The 2011 Yellow Pages lists eighteen Asian Indian restaurants and at least one Asian Indian grocery store in and around the city. However, technology sectors attract most Asian Indians, and they fill a crucial gap in the city's labor markets. Biotechnology and tech-based agriculture, such as ethanol production, draw Asian Indians as does e-business. According to a Duke University study, Asian Indians founded more tech start-up companies in the United States than any other foreign-born group from 1995 through 2005.

Rajan Gajaria, from Dow AgroSciences and the Board of Directors of the International Center of Indianapolis, states that Asian Indians are drawn to Indiana and its capital city because of the high quality of life, the low cost of living, the excellent colleges and universities, and the relatively low cost of conducting business. He also speaks favorably

Indian American Kanwal Prakash "K. P." Singh holds up his passport while explaining that since 9/11 he is sometimes questioned because of his turban, and he keeps his passport with him to show his American citizenship. Singh was among the first Asian Indians to live in Indianapolis. Having trained in India and the United States as an artist and architect, he came to Indianapolis in 1967 as the city's senior urban planner. Singh has been a force in the preservation of Indianapolis's historic places such as Union Station, as well as serving as a cultural ambassador for new immigrants from his home country.

of the growing diversity in Indianapolis and the growing acceptance by Hoosiers for its immigrant populations.

Gajaria's comments contrast starkly with descriptions of Indiana from a century ago. One immigrant who has witnessed the changes since the 1960s is Kanwal Prakash Singh of India, one of Indianapolis's earliest Asian Indian residents. An architect and artist, trained in India and the United States, Singh moved to Indianapolis when he became the senior urban planner for the Department of Metropolitan Development in 1967. In 1972 he began his firm, K. P. Singh Designs, specializing in fine art and design. Since then, he has won many awards for his community efforts, particularly in historic preservation, including helping to save Indianapolis's Union Station. He was the founding president of the International Center of Indianapolis and works to communicate across cultures about cultural and spiritual matters as well as about history and architecture. In June 2011 Singh was awarded the Hoosier Heritage Lifetime Achievement Award from Heritage Place in Indianapolis. Singh takes much joy in the influx of immigrants to Indiana in the twenty-first century, celebrating the rich heritage each group brings to the Hoosier heartland.

Asian Indian Hoosiers bring a rich variety of religious and cultural traditions. In Indianapolis Asian Indians belong to spiritual traditions of Hinduism, Sikhism, Buddhism, Judaism, Christianity, Islam, and others. They live in the suburban areas of Indianapolis, not in ethnic enclaves, and come together socially with other American professionals or at the India Community Center at West 56th Street and Guion Road. Asian Indians of all backgrounds and faiths also celebrate Diwali, the Festival of Lights, in places across the city, with hundreds of Asian Indians and other Indianapolis residents. Originally a Hindu festival celebrating the triumph of light over darkness/good over evil, Diwali has been adopted by Asian Indian Hoosiers as a way to celebrate their pan-Indian heritage in their new country of choice.

Indian Americans Rajinderbir Singh Bhullar of Denver and Navjeet Bhullar of Indianapolis were married in a traditional Sikh ceremony at the Gurdwara Sahib of Indianapolis near Acton in November 2007.

Muslims gather for prayer inside the Islamic Society of North America Mosque in Plainfield, Indiana, during services to mark Eid-al-Fitr at the conclusion of the month of Ramadan in September 2010.

Indianapolis Welcomes Its Southern Neighbors

Hispanics Become Hoosiers

Just as the Diwali festival has been transformed in America to celebrate Asian Indian heritage, so too has Cinco de Mayo become a day to celebrate Hispanic heritage in the United States. On May 5, 1862, Mexican troops, many of them armed only with machetes, defeated French invading forces in the First Battle of Puebla. The second battle, a year later, drew in forces from California, many of them immigrants from Central and South America. According to a source at the University of California at Los Angeles, it was these immigrant Americans who started the tradition of Cinco de Mayo in California to celebrate the initial victory. Since 1863 this celebration has spread across the nation. Today, Indianapolis residents join with Americans across the country, enjoying Latin American food, music, and beer on Cinco de Mayo.

The spread of this celebration happened in concert with increasing Hispanic immigration into the United States. From 2000 to 2006 immigration numbers rose dramatically in Indiana as in the country, the largest proportion coming from Mexico. Although the number of immigrants appears to have declined during the recent recession, in 2000 there were less than 215,000 Hispanics in Indiana, while in 2009 there were nearly 390,000. Marion County's numbers rose even faster, jumping from 33,000 to 84,000 within these few years. While the largest percentage of Hoosier Hispanics come from Mexico, substantial numbers also come from Puerto Rico, whose residents are U.S. citizens, and Cuba, whose refugees from Fidel Castro's communist dictatorship continue to flee to America. The following countries are also represented in

Indianapolis: Argentina, Chile, Colombia, Dominican Republic, El Salvador, Guatemala, Honduras, Peru, and Venezuela.

Just as other recent immigrants, Hispanics are drawn to America as "the land of opportunity." They wish to have a better life for themselves and their families, and they realize that they will be much more likely to succeed in the United States than in their home countries, which present varying economic and political challenges. Here again, Indiana provides a particular draw because of its friendly business environment, high quality of life, low cost of living, and the welcome it displays to newcomers. More than twenty-four nonprofit organizations serve Indianapolis's Hispanic population. One of the oldest and largest is La Plaza, which serves people by "providing education, health, and

Map of the Latin American nations, circa 2003.

Reunion of La Plaza staff, 2009. La Plaza serves the Hispanic community in and around Indianapolis through education programs and health and social services. Currently its staff includes individuals from Mexico, Puerto Rico, Santo Domingo, and Venezuela as well as people who have studied and/or lived in Latin America or Spain. Longtime executive director, Miriam Acevedo Davis (fourth from right in back), hails from Puerto Rico.

These students, part of La Plaza's Tu Futuro Program, volunteered at the 2009 Santa Comes to Town holiday assistance/ health fair event.

social services, and business and economic development support while also sharing the richness of the arts and culture of Latinos with the Indianapolis community." In addition, in 2005 the Indianapolis Chamber of Commerce joined with the city's Hispanic Chamber of Commerce to form the Hispanic Business Council.

Hispanic immigrants tend to be less educated than their Asian and Middle Eastern counterparts. Many have not finished high school. Consequently, more of them work in less-lucrative jobs in wholesale, retail, distribution, food services, construction, manufacturing, hotels, landscaping, and farming. A smaller proportion of them work in professional or technical capacities, such as in the medical field.

Indiana has long drawn on Hispanics to fill out its workforce. After World War I, Indiana's northern steel mills recruited Mexicans. Migrant workers from Central and South America traveled to Indiana to harvest fruits and vegetables starting in the mid-twentieth century, comprising nearly a quarter of the state's farm labor. Eli Lilly and Company also brought some Latin American pharmaceutical professionals to Indianapolis during these years.

Many migrant workers found employment in cities such as Indianapolis and eventually moved here. One such man was Jesus "Jesse" Quintana. Born in Mexico in 1928, he moved to Texas and was married during the 1940s. Quintana obtained legal immigrant status in 1950. Working as a farm laborer, he traveled to Indiana. When bad weather left him jobless, Quintana came to Indianapolis and was quickly hired by the Indianapolis Union Railway. From 1952 through 1969 Quintana worked at a burial vault manufacturing company. Thereafter, he worked for lumber companies and a roofing company until 1980 when he retired.

Quintana took English and citizenship classes to become a U.S. citizen. Although he had only a fifth-grade education from Mexico, he passed his tests and was naturalized in 1958.

Quintana played guitar in bands at Indianapolis's Latin American clubs and restaurants. During his retirement he played at schools and festivals as well.

The Parade of Flags at FIESTA Indianapolis recognizes the twenty Spanish-speaking countries of Latin America (and Brazil and Spain). The central Indiana Hispanic community includes people from Mexico, Cuba, Colombia, Argentina, and other countries.

Five of Quintana's sons served in the military during the Korean and Vietnam Wars. In 1990 one was a teacher in Indianapolis, another was a postal worker, a third was a supervisor at a Veterans Hospital in California, and Quintana's daughter worked for a loan company in Greenwood, Indiana.

Many from Indianapolis's Hispanic community, such as the Quintanas, belong to Saint Mary or Saint Patrick Catholic parishes just east of downtown Indianapolis. These parishes offer Mass in Spanish. Many join Protestant churches as well. In 1998 there were Spanish-speaking churches from the following denominations near downtown or on the city's east side: Baptist, Disciples of Christ, Jehovah's Witnesses, United Methodist, Pentecostal, and nondenominational.

One Protestant Mexican American, whose story began in the impoverished region of Hidalgo, Mexico, is Juana Watson. Watson immigrated to Columbus, Indiana, in 1978, the bride of a Cummins executive. Before she became a U.S. citizen in

La Plaza promotes physical education through many of its programs. Pictured here are children playing futbol in La Plaza's Summer Discovery Program. This game, known as soccer in the United States, is popular throughout Latin America and the world.

1996, she raised her three children and began her life's work—helping new immigrants thrive and fostering education and understanding between the people of her first and chosen homes. Through the Friends of Hidalgo, a nonprofit organization that Watson started, twenty members of her Columbus church traveled with her to her birth village in 1991. Eventually, visitors included high school and college students, doctors, dentists, Indianapolis police officers, firefighters, and social workers as well as Mayor Bart Peterson and Lieutenant Governor Becky Skillman. Today, Indiana University–Purdue University, Indianapolis students and faculty travel each year to Hidalgo to give much-needed care to area residents while gaining invaluable firsthand experience with Latin American patients.

Watson's journey has been rewarding. After learning English and earning a high school diploma, she earned a bachelor's degree in Tourism Management from IUPUI (1999), a master's of Latin American–Caribbean Studies at IU Bloomington (2005), and a doctorate of education from the Graduate Theological Foundation (2008). She also founded or cofounded the following organizations: Su Casa Columbus Hispanic/Latino Center; Badges without Borders,

SOL (Student Organization of Latinos) is a group from Ivy Tech that does volunteer work at FIESTA Indianapolis each year. La Plaza's education programs promote postsecondary education for Hispanics, taking students from elementary through high school and their parents on college visits throughout Indiana.

a law-enforcement exchange program; the Indiana Multi-Ethnic Conference; and Indiana Diversity Women's Network. Watson was an adviser for Governor Mitch Daniels and the Institute of Mexicans Abroad and served on the Indiana Hispanic Latino Commission and as president of the consulting firm Eye 2 the World. Having won many awards, she is currently a college professor, motivational speaker, and storyteller.

Watson's work helps Hispanic entrepreneurs who come to Indianapolis to start businesses as well as children and grandchildren of Indiana's early Hispanic immigrants. In 2007 there were more than 8,500 Hispanic-owned businesses in Indiana, which employed more than 14,000 people, with sales of $1.7 billion. In 2010 the purchasing power of the state's Hispanics totaled $7.8 billion. Similar

Juana Watson at the Mexican Consulate in downtown Indianapolis, 2009.

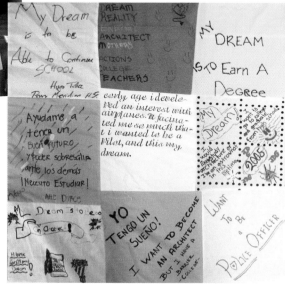

The Latino/a Youth Collective provides resources and opportunities for young people to engage in personal and community development. Since 2006 members have been sewing a DREAM quilt, with students' goals and dreams, representing the immigrant community's hope and power. Holding more than one thousand squares, it has been replicated countrywide.

to most other immigrant children, most of the children of Hispanic immigrants are born and educated here. Consequently, they are generally better educated than their parents and work in every sector and at all levels of Indiana's economy.

A Twenty-first-Century City
The Indianapolis Mosaic

Twenty-first-century Indianapolis is blessed with food from around the world. One can readily find Mexican, Chinese, Indian, Greek, Jewish, Cajun, French, German, and Italian restaurants, and there are individual restaurants for Cuban, Ethiopian, and other ethnic foods. Walking in the city's downtown one can see turbans and saris alongside baseball caps and business suits. Throughout the year there are festivals for different ethnic groups; and each fall the Nationalities Council of Indiana hosts an International Festival, which "introduces thousands of schoolchildren and adults to the city's wide range of culinary, historical, social, ethnic, and linguistic heritages."

Despite these celebrations and the city's many government, business, and nonprofit organizations that serve ethnic populations, many immigrants—legal as well as illegal—feel uncertain about their future in America. The recent influx of immigrants, mainly from Mexico, India, and China, as well as the recent economic recession have brought immigration issues to a political head. Speaking loudly through news outlets and sometimes with pickets, some Americans insist that immigrants should go home and quit taking American jobs and that the U.S. government should stop using tax dollars for education and social services to immigrants, especially illegal immigrants.

Today's speeches echo sentiments from the early twentieth century when Ku Klux Klan members and others worked successfully to severely limit immigration; and they sound similar to the nineteenth-century rhetoric of Americans who wanted to stop the Irish, Germans, and Chinese from coming to the United States and to send all blacks back to Africa. In similar ways, Mexicans, Asians, and Middle Easterners are made to feel unwanted in their new land.

Although discrimination appears to be part of the story of all immigrant groups, many Indianapolis

Cousins Igor Minevich, ten (left) and Sasha Kotlyar, thirteen, both students at the Hasten Hebrew Academy of Indianapolis, surveyed the crowd as they waited for the start of a Passover Seder at the Congregation B'Nai Torah synagogue. The religious feast was held for nearly two hundred Russian Jewish immigrants in 1998.

citizens believe it is detrimental to the city. Indianapolis businesses are recruiting workers around the world. Meanwhile, organizations such as the Greater Indianapolis Chamber of Commerce are working to make immigrants feel welcome to ensure that central Indiana can compete in the twenty-first century's global marketplace.

In fact, the United States would suffer economically without immigrants—both legal and illegal. Immigrants helped to build this nation and still help to build it. According to a 1990s bipartisan Congressional study, immigration increases the labor supply, helping to bring the most capable people to places where there are jobs requiring their skills—from entry-level through professional positions.

The increased labor supply from legal and illegal immigrants helps provide goods and services at lower costs to American consumers and contributes from $1 to $10 billion to the gross domestic product each year. Additionally, since the majority of immigrants are young, they pay local, state,

Dancers from the Indianapolis Chinese Performing Arts end their performance at the second annual Asian Festival presented by the Asian American Alliance and Indy Parks and Recreation at Garfield Park in May 2009.

federal, and sales taxes for decades, adding greatly to government coffers. Even when expenses for education and social services, such as Medicare, are subtracted from the taxes immigrants pay, their paid taxes outweigh their expense, according to the bipartisan study.

Moreover, the children and grandchildren of immigrants attain higher levels of education and better-paying jobs than preceding generations, adding enhanced levels of productivity, spending power, and taxes to the economy. For immigrants who stay, the story usually brightens in other ways, too. While new immigrants often struggle with language issues and hold tight to traditions from their homelands,

their children grasp English more easily, adapt to living within both their ethnic and the wider American culture, and often move into wider social circles than their parents.

During the process of assimilation into American culture, large groups, such as the Germans and Chinese, usually form culture clubs where they share the food, music, crafts, and stories from their homelands. Smaller groups, whose first affinities are to a tiny village rather than to a state such as Hungary, may join with villagers from the region they called home, forming panethnic associations. These latter groups may choose symbolic foods, songs, dances, and even costumes to stand for the variety of cultural icons each village cherished in order to celebrate their similar cultures together. In Indianapolis, organizations such as the India Community Center exemplify this phenomenon.

A young girl paints Easter eggs, an activity enjoyed throughout the Western world for centuries.

Most immigrants share a concern for relatives they left behind in "the old country." American immigrants send billions of dollars of money and goods to their home countries each year. This charitable impulse extends to newcomers from their homelands. Immigrants, either individually or through ethnic associations, have traditionally housed, fed, and clothed new immigrants, helped them find jobs, and assisted them in navigating their new land.

To most immigrants, a religious community becomes very important. A faith system helps connect the old and new lives of immigrants. Also, the building provides a place to meet others of a similar background, who are working through similar experiences.

Immigrants often staunchly defend America. They support freedom, equal opportunity, civil rights, and building a better life through hard work. Throughout American history immigrants have fought alongside other Americans to defend these ideals. Consequently, Indianapolis is home to American veterans from countries around the world as well as Native American veterans.

Dancers from the Anderson (Indiana) Ballet Folklorico perform traditional Mexican dances in costume each year at FIESTA Indianapolis.

Indiana's Native Americans were forced to leave the state because the earliest Hoosiers disagreed with their communal way of life. After nearly two centuries, Indianapolis is gaining a reputation for welcoming people from around the world who bring many different ways of life to the city—including the first people who lived on American soil. In the twenty-first century, people from across Indiana, the United States, and countries around the world live together in Indianapolis, creating a mosaic of rich colors, tastes, and sounds, a city with opportunities for all.

Photo of Indiana Multiethnic Committee Conference participants in Indianapolis in 2008. This grassroots committee was formed in 2007 to help make Indiana a more welcoming place for newcomers by bringing people and organizations together to share resources and ideas, to help educate the public about changing demographics and globalization, and to research and maintain current information on multiethnic Indiana.

Indianapolis's Immigrant Welcome Center

As immigration increased at the beginning of the twenty-first century—with the encouragement of Indianapolis's business community—the city's first lady, Amy Peterson, led a research group in 2005 that focused on immigrants' needs. The group decided to create an organization in which community members would help new immigrants, similar to a program in Seattle, Washington. Thus was born the Immigrant Welcome Center of Indianapolis, a nonprofit organization that welcomes immigrants and helps them establish roots in the city. Through volunteers called "Natural Helpers" and community partners, the Center "connects newcomers to the resources, services, and opportunities they need to fully participate in the economic, civic, social and cultural life of the community."

Natural Helpers are volunteers living or working in immigrant communities that newcomers would naturally go to for help. Each one is at least bilingual, has attended a Helpers training program, and attends bimonthly workshops. Many of them

were U.S. immigrants at one time or have some related experience, so they can relate easily to new immigrants.

The Center enjoys partnerships with many organizations in the city, especially its funders: Reuben Family Foundation, Efroymson Family Fund, Clowes Fund, Nina Mason Pulliam Charitable Trust, and Nicholas H. Noyes Jr. Memorial Foundation. More than fifty other organizations support the Welcome Center, so that immigrants can obtain assistance with health care; legal, social, employment, and training services; government agencies; public transportation, education, and safety resources; housing, financial aid; and other needs.

The Center also collects information about how to best meet immigrant needs, coordinates inter-agency services, and addresses barriers to access. Its small staff and volunteers are guided by a board of directors, many of whom "work with or represent immigrant, refugee, and newcomer populations."

To learn more about the Welcome Center of Indianapolis, consult its website, http://www.immigrantwelcomecenter.org/, or call (317) 808-2326.

The Immigrant Welcome Center of Indianapolis helps immigrants from around the world become familiar with the city as it becomes their new home.

Indianapolis Neighborhood Map

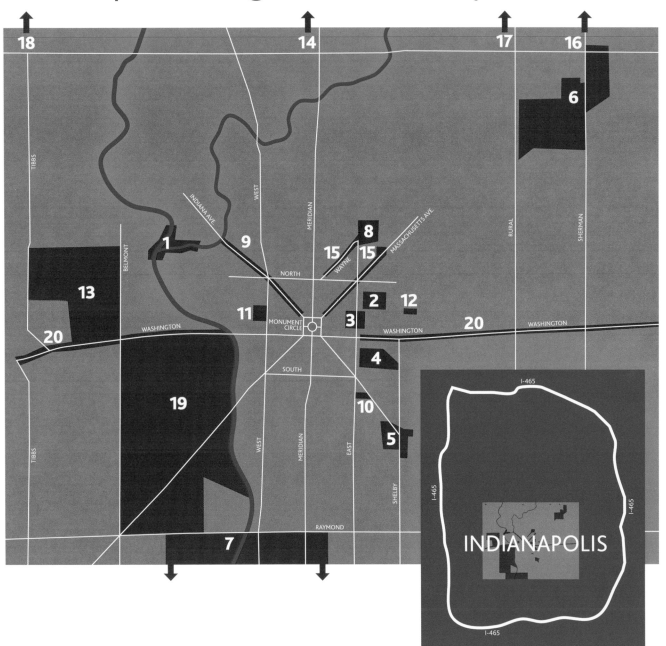

1

Mouth of Fall Creek: Commissioners appointed by the Indiana legislature in Corydon decided to relocate the state's capital near this place where Fall Creek empties into the west fork of the White River.

2 & 3

Lockerbie Square & Germantown: The area around Lockerbie Street, just northeast of the Circle in downtown Indianapolis, was an early home of Americans of Scottish and Scots-Irish descent. They were among the earliest settlers in the capital city. By the mid-nineteenth century, German immigrants were also making a home in the area just south of Lockerbie, which became known as Germantown.

4 & 5

Irish Hill & Fountain Square: The neighborhoods known as Irish Hill and Fountain Square became home to many Irish immigrants during the nineteenth century. Many eastern and southern Europeans also lived in Fountain Square beginning near the turn of the twentieth century. After World War II a new influx of immigrants from the upper South, particularly Kentucky and Tennessee, moved into these and other south, west, and east side neighborhoods.

6

Brightwood: Brightwood was a large neighborhood that grew up around the foundries, or railroad shops, of the Bee Line Railroad Company. The neighborhood was home to many of the families who worked in the shops, including numerous immigrants from England, Ireland, and Germany.

7

German Gardeners Benefit Society: In 1867 German immigrants on the city's south side formed a society to organize the sale of produce from their many "truck gardens," that is, fruit and vegetables grown in greenhouses and trucked to marketplaces all over the city.

8

Chatham–Arch: This neighborhood just north of Fort Wayne Avenue was a home to several early African American families. Over time, however, German American shopkeepers and professionals became the primary inhabitants.

9

Indiana Avenue: Although African Americans originally settled on Indianapolis's near south side, by the 1880s most had moved to the area surrounding Indiana Avenue. The avenue boasted the black commercial district, including the *Indianapolis Recorder* newspaper. During the first half of the twentieth century, Indiana Avenue was famous for its jazz music scene. In ensuing years, blacks inhabited neighborhoods from Washington Street to Forty-sixth Street. Similar to other ethnic groups, today well-educated blacks tend to live in Indianapolis's suburbs.

10

Holy Rosary Catholic Church: Holy Rosary Catholic Church was instituted for Italian Americans in Indianapolis between 1911 and 1925. Since the 1980s the church has hosted an annual Italian street festival, drawing up to 25,000 visitors in recent years.

11 & 12

Military Park & Highland Park: Many Greek immigrants lived near Holy Trinity Greek Orthodox Church during the first part of the twentieth century—around Highland Park (east of the Circle) and Military Park (west of the Circle). Today, Holy Trinity Greek Orthodox Church is in Carmel.

13

Haughville: West of White River and north of Washington Street, the neighborhood of Haughville arose and grew as eastern and southern Europeans, including Slovenes and Hungarians, poured into the west side of Indianapolis during the first part of the twentieth century. Many African Americans and Hispanic Americans reside there today as well.

14

Indianapolis Hebrew Congregation & JCC: Nineteenth-century German Jewish immigrants tended to live on the near south side, while eastern European Jews lived among the ethnic groups they immigrated with. In the twentieth century, many Jewish people moved to northern Marion County, establishing the Indianapolis Hebrew Congregation and the Jewish Community Center.

15

Fort Wayne and Massachusetts Avenues: Prior to the twentieth century, Indianapolis's meager Chinese population lived and worked along Fort Wayne and Massachusetts Avenues. Today, Asian Americans live throughout the Indianapolis area with concentrations in Carmel and Fishers on the north side, around West Thirty-eighth Street, and in Perry Township on the south side.

16

Saint George Orthodox Christian Church: Christian Syrians and Lebanese who emmigrated from the Middle East around the turn of the twentieth century established Saint George Church north of Thirty-eighth Street on East Sherman Drive. There are plans in 2012 to sell this building and move the church north to Fishers.

17

Islamic Center & Islamic bookstore: Muslims from Middle Eastern countries, who have been coming to Indianapolis the last few decades, live throughout the city and its suburbs. They have opened cultural establishments north of downtown and on the south side, including the headquarters of the Islamic Society of North America, which is a mosque in Plainfield. There is also an Islamic Center started by the nation of Islam, an African American group, as well as an Islamic bookstore near Saint George Orthodox Christian Church on the northeast side of town.

18

India Community Center: Similar to other immigrants who have moved to Indianapolis in the last few decades, Asian Indians are dispersed throughout the city and many reside in the northern suburbs of Zionsville, Carmel, and Fishers. The India Association of Indianapolis owns a community center near Fifty-sixth Street and Guion Road.

19 & 20

West Indianapolis & Washington Street Corridors: Hispanics, who have been moving into Indianapolis since the latter half of the twentieth century, live across the town and its suburbs, with one of several concentrations in west Indianapolis. While they have developed distinctive business districts along the west and east sides of Washington Street, Mexican restaurants flourish throughout Marion County.

Time Line of Immigrant Arrivals into Indianapolis

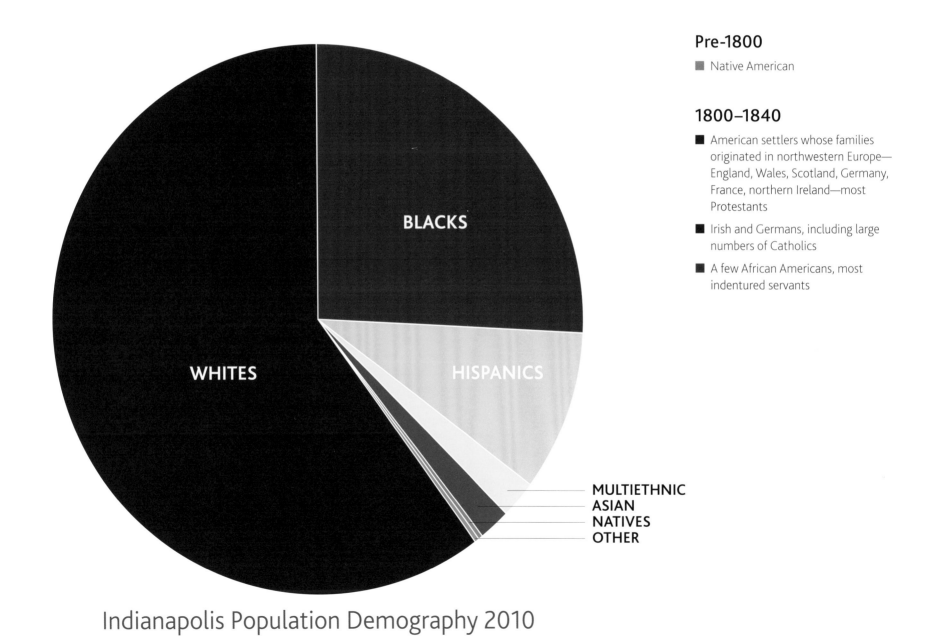

Indianapolis Population Demography 2010

Pre-1800

■ Native American

1800–1840

■ American settlers whose families originated in northwestern Europe— England, Wales, Scotland, Germany, France, northern Ireland—most Protestants

■ Irish and Germans, including large numbers of Catholics

■ A few African Americans, most indentured servants

1840–Civil War

- German-speaking people from north-western Europe, including Protestants, Catholics, and Jews
- Others from northwestern Europe
- African Americans—free blacks and escaped slaves
- A few individuals from Canada, Italy, and Switzerland

Mid-1860s–1880

- African Americans—newly freed slaves and former free blacks
- German-speaking people from northwestern Europe, including Protestants, Catholics, and Jews
- Others from northwestern Europe
- Very few individuals from other ethnic groups

1880s–1920

- People from southeastern Europe, particularly Greece, Hungary, Italy, Poland, and Russia, including Slavic people such as Slovenes, many Catholics and Jews
- African Americans from southern states
- A few individuals from China
- Christians and Jews from Syria and individuals from other Middle Eastern countries
- A few individuals from Mexico

1920s–1930s

- African Americans from southern states
- Refugees from eastern and southern Europe, including Jews and others from Russia, Ukraine, Czechoslovakia, Latvia, Lithuania, Poland, Romania, and Yugoslavia
- Mexican migrant workers
- Little foreign immigration otherwise due to anti-immigration laws federally and racial discrimination locally

1940–1980s

- African Americans
- Japanese Americans released from U.S. internment camps during World War II
- Jews escaping Holocaust
- Refugees from Communist Cuba
- Refugees from Soviet Union
- War refugees and students from Korea, many Protestant
- War refugees from Vietnam, Cambodia, and Laos, many Buddhist or Hindu
- Filipinos, most highly educated professionals
- Well-educated Asian Indians of many faiths, including Sikhism, Hinduism, and Buddhism
- Uneducated Mexican laborers, most Catholic
- Native Americans from 150 different tribes
- Students, professionals, and technical workers from Egypt, Syria, Turkey, Lebanon, and several other Middle Eastern countries, many Islamic

1990–Present

- Large numbers of poorly educated Mexicans and other Hispanics, most Catholic, some Protestant, most laborers and small business owners
- Well-educated Asian Indians, many working in technical fields
- Asians, particularly Chinese, Japanese, Filipinos, Koreans, and Vietnamese
- African Americans
- Native Americans
- People from the Middle East, particularly Turkey, Egypt, and Syria, many Islamic
- People from African countries
- Other individuals from across the globe

Photograph credits

Selected Bibliography

Archives, Libraries, and Research Facilities

Aponte, Robert. "Latinos in Indiana: On the Throes of Growth," Statistical Brief no. 11, July 1999. Julian Samora Research Institute, Michigan State University, East Lansing, MI. http://www.jsri.msu.edu/.

———. "Latinos in Indiana: Growth, Distribution, and Implications," Statistical Brief no. 14, August 2002. Julian Samora Research Institute, Michigan State University, East Lansing, MI. http://www.jsri.msu.edu/.

Bartlett, Lauren. "Cinco de Mayo Observance Is Important Because It Provides a Collective Identity for Latinos, Says UCLA Center." UCLA Newsroom, May 4, 2007. http://newsroom.ucla.edu/portal/ucla/Cinco-de-Mayo-Observance-Is-Important-7891.aspx.

Braziel, Jana Evans. "History of Migration and Immigration Laws in the United States." Spring 2000. On ACLAnet (American Comparative Literature Association). http://www.umass.edu/complit/aclanet/USMigrat.html.

Burger, Janice McCracken. Phone interview with Wendy L. Adams, Indiana Historical Society Press, May 2011.

Conner, Nancy Nakano. "Japanese and Japanese Americans in Indiana." Text of exhibit module from "Bridges to Japan." Indianapolis: Indiana State Fair, August 2010.

Deal, Shirley. Phone interview with Wendy L. Adams, Indiana Historical Society Press, May 2011.

Diebold, Paul. "Indianapolis: Discover Our Shared Heritage Travel Itinerary." http://www.nps.gov/history/nr/travel/indianapolis/index.htm.

Esipova, Neli, Julie Ray, and Rajesh Srinivasan. "Young, Less Educated Yearn to Migrate to the US: Canada More Attractive to Older, More Educated Adults." Gallup, April 30, 2010. http://www.gallup.com/home.aspx.

Ferguson, Earline Rae. "A Community Affair: African-American Women's Club Work in Indianapolis, 1879–1917." PhD diss., Indiana University, 1997.

Harvard University Library Open Collections Program. "Aspiration, Acculturation, and Impact: Immigration to the United States, 1789–1930." http://ocp.hul.harvard.edu/immigration/.

Heet, Justin, and Courtney Burkey, John Clark, and David G. Vanderstel. "The Impact of Immigration on Indiana: A Series of Briefing Papers Prepared by the Sagamore Institute for Policy Research." Indianapolis: Sagamore Institute for Policy Research, February 2009. http://www.sagamoreinstitute.org/mediafiles/impact-of-immigration.pdf.

Hirschman, Charles. "The Impact of Immigration on American Society: Looking Backward to the Future." In "Border Battles: The U.S. Immigration Debates." Brooklyn, NY: Social Science Research Council, July 28, 2006. http://borderbattles.ssrc.org/.

Immigration Policy Center. "New Americans in Indiana." In "The Economic and Political Impact of Immigrants, Latinos, and Asians, State by State." Washington, DC: American Immigration Council, January 12, 2012.

Indiana Department of Natural Resources, Division of Historic Preservation and Archaeology. "Marion County History." http://www.in.gov/dnr/historic/files/marion_jewish.pdf.

Indiana Historical Bureau. "Black Settlers in Indiana." *The Indiana Junior Historian*. Indianapolis, 1993.

Indianapolis Historic Preservation Commission. "Historic Areas of Indianapolis—Marion County" map. Indianapolis, June 1977.

Indiana University Center, IU News Room. "Indiana Census Results Show Population Gains and Losses All over the Map" and "Indiana's Census Shows Increasing Diversity." Bloomington: Indiana University, February 10, 2011. http://newsinfo.iu.edu/news/page/normal/17318.html.

Indiana University–Purdue University, Indianapolis, Max Kade German–American Center. "The German–Americans of Indianapolis." IUPUI University Libraries. http://www.ulib.iupui.edu/kade/indianapolis.html.

Kinghorn, Matt. "Recession Alters Indiana Migration Trends." *Incontext* 9, no. 4 (April 2008). Indiana Business Research Center, Indiana University Kelley School of Business. http://www.incontext.indiana.edu/2010/may-june/article1.asp.

Latham, Charles. "Harvey N. Middleton Papers, 1928–1978 (M 0441)." Collection guide. Indianapolis: Indiana Historical Society, 2004. http://www.indianahistory.org/our-collections/collection-guides/harvey-n-middleton-papers-1928-1978.pdf.

Lindseth, Erik L., and Gregory H. Mobley. "Athenaeum Turners Records, 1880–2002." Collection guide. IUPUI University Library Special Collections and Archives, Indiana University–Purdue University, Indianapolis, November 2000.

Middleton, Harvey Nathaniel. "Autobiography." Box A, Folders 1 and 2, Harvey N. Middleton Papers, 1928–1978, M 0441. William Henry Smith Memorial Library, Indiana Historical Society, Indianapolis, Indiana.

Mobley, Gregory H. "American Turners Records, 1853–2004." Collection guide. Ruth Lilly Special Collections and Archives, Indiana University–Purdue University, Indianapolis, April 2002.

The Polis Center. "Study Neighborhoods from the Project on Religion and Urban Culture." http://www.polis.iupui.edu/RUC/Neighborhoods/.

Quintana, Jesus "Jesse." Interview with Charles Guthrie, University of Indianapolis, March 12, 1990. Interview 1 of Hispanic Indianapolis Oral History Project. Transcribed by Dan Briere. Typescript in Hispanic Indianapolis: Personal Histories from an Emerging Community, Oral History Project, 1990, BV 3516–3525, William Henry Smith Memorial Library, Indiana Historical Society, Indianapolis, Indiana.

Rios, Jesus, and Steve Crabtree. "One in Four Latin Americans Wishes to Emigrate: United States Named as Preferred Destination by 33%," January 21, 2008. Gallup. http://www.gallup.com/poll/103837/One-Four-Latin-Americans-Wishes-Emigrate.aspx/.

———. "Latin Americans' Motives for Migration: Poverty, Unemployment Fail to Provide Complete Picture," January 23, 2008. Gallup. http://www.gallup.com/poll/103837/Latin-Americans-Motives-Migration.aspx/

———. "Ambition and Emigration among Latin Americans: Those Who Are Driven to Succeed More Likely to Want to Emigrate," February 4, 2008. Gallup. http://www.gallup.com/poll/103837/Ambition-Emigration-Latin-Americans.aspx.

Sarabia, Jenny. "Educational Challenges and Opportunities Faced by Latinos in Indiana—Indianapolis as a Case Study." Indianapolis: Commission on Hispanic/Latino Affairs, 2004. http://www.in.gov/ichla/files/2004_Education_Report.pdf.

Singer, Audrey, and Jill H. Wilson. "The Impact of the Great Recession on Metropolitan Immigration Trends." Metropolitan Policy Program at Brookings, December 2010. http://www.brookings.edu/metro.

Stats Indiana: Data Everyone Can Use. Indianapolis: Indiana Business Research Center, Kelley School of Business, Indiana University, with support from State of Indiana, Lilly Endowment, and Indiana Department of Workforce Development. http://www.stats.indiana.edu/index.asp.

Souchet-Moura, Katherine. Phone interview and e-mail exchanges with M. Teresa Baer, Indiana Historical Society Press, March and April 2012.

US Census Bureau:

American Community Survey. http://www.census.gov/acs/.

American Fact Finder. http://factfinder2.census.gov/.

Censtats Databases. "2010 Census: Indiana Profile"; "Indiana: 2000: Census 2000 Profile." August 2002.

Census 2000 Briefs and Special Reports. "The Arab Population: 2000: Census 2000 Brief." http://www.census.gov/prod/2003pubs/c2kbr-23.pdf.

Census '90. "Congressional Districts of the 103rd Congress: Table 3. Sex, Race, and Hispanic Origin: 1990 (Indiana)." http://censtats.census.gov/.

Quick Facts. http://quickfacts.census.gov/.

"State and County Quick Facts: Indiana," November 4, 2010.

"State and County Quick Facts: Indianapolis (City [Balance]), Indiana," October 18, 2011.

"State and County Quick Facts: Marion County, Indiana," October 13, 2011.

"US Federal Census Collection." Transcribed, indexed, and digitized records from US Census Bureau data, 1790–1930, from microfilm from National Archives and Records Administration, Washington, DC. Provo, UT: Ancestry.com/. http://search.ancestry.com/.

Books

Adams, Willi Paul. *The German Americans: An Ethnic Experience*. American ed. Translated and adapted by LaVern J. Rippley and Eberhard Reichmann. New York: Max Kade German-American Center, Indiana University–Purdue University, Indianapolis, with the support of the German Information Center, 1993.

The Alpha Home Story: Yesterday, Today, Tomorrow. Indianapolis: The Alpha Home Association of Greater Indianapolis, [1973?].

Blanchard, Charles. *History of the Catholic Church in Indiana*. 2 vols. Logansport, IN: A. W. Bowen and Company, 1898.

Bodenhamer, David J., and Robert G. Barrows, eds. *The Encyclopedia of Indianapolis*. Bloomington and Indianapolis: Indiana University Press, 1994.

Divita, James J. *Slaves to No One: A History of the Holy Trinity Catholic Community in Indianapolis on the Diamond Jubilee of the Founding of Holy Trinity Parish*. [Indianapolis]: Holy Trinity Parish with the cooperation of the Ethnic History Project, Indiana Historical Society, 1981.

Dunn, Jacob Piatt, Jr. *Greater Indianapolis: The History, the Industries, the Institutions, and the People of a City of Homes*. 2 vols. Chicago: Lewis Publishing, 1910.

———. *Indiana and Indianans: A History of Aboriginal and Territorial Indiana and the Century of Statehood*. 5 vols. Chicago: American Historical Society, 1919.

Gibbs, Wilma L., ed. *Indiana's African–American Heritage: Essays from* Black History News & Notes. Indianapolis: Indiana Historical Society, 1993.

Giffin, William W. *The Irish*. Peopling Indiana, vol. 1. Indianapolis: Indiana Historical Society Press, 2006.

Glenn, Elizabeth, and Stewart Rafert. *The Native Americans*. Peopling Indiana, vol. 2. Indianapolis: Indiana Historical Society Press, 2009.

Hine, Darlene Clark. *When the Truth Is Told: A History of Black Women's Culture and Community in Indiana, 1875–1950*. [Indianapolis]: The National Council of Negro Women, Indianapolis Section, 1981.

Phillips, Clifton J. *Indiana in Transition: The Emergence of an Industrial Commonwealth, 1880–1920*. History of Indiana, vol. 4. Indianapolis: Indiana Historical Bureau and Indiana Historical Society, 1968.

Polk's Indianapolis (Marion County, Ind.) City Directory. Indianapolis: R. L. Polk and Co., 1900s–1973.

Probst, George T., and Eberhard Reichmann. *The Germans in Indianapolis, 1840–1918*. Indianapolis: German–American Center, Indiana University–Purdue University, Indianapolis, and Indiana German Heritage Society, 1989.

Rafert, Stewart. *The Miami Indians of Indiana: A Persistent People, 1654–1994*. Indianapolis: Indiana Historical Society, 1996.

Sherman, John, and Jeffrey A. Wolin. *New Faces at the Crossroads: The World in Central Indiana*. Bloomington: International Center of Indianapolis in association with Indiana University Press, 2007.

Sisson, Richard, Christian K. Zacher, and Andrew Robert Lee Cayton, eds. *The American Midwest: An Interpretive Encyclopedia*. Bloomington: Indiana University Press, 2007.

Smith, James P., and Barry Edmonston, eds. *The New Americans: Economic, Demographic, and Fiscal Effects of Immigration*. Washington, DC: National Academy Press, 1997.

Sulgrove, Berry R. *History of Indianapolis and Marion County, Indiana*. Philadelphia: L. H. Everts and Company, 1884.

Taylor, Robert M., and Connie A. McBirney, eds. *Peopling Indiana: The Ethnic Experience*. Indianapolis: Indiana Historical Society, 1996.

Periodicals

Born, Cathy. "The Indianapolis Gardeners Benefit Society: German American Truck Farmers and Greenhouse Growers on the City's South Side, 1867–2009." *The Hoosier Genealogist: Connections* 49, no. 1 (Spring/Summer 2009): 57–61.

Carpenter, Dan. "Inclusion and Exclusion: Indiana's Chinese Community." *The Hoosier Genealogist* 41, no. 4 (December 2001): 206–15.

"Congregations and Immigrant Communities." *Religion & Community*, 4, no. 1 (Fall 1998). http://www.polis.iupui.edu/RUC/Newsletters/Religion/vol4no1.htm.

Conner, Nancy Nakano. "From Internment to Indiana: Japanese Americans, the War Relocation Authority, the Disciples of Christ, and Citizen Committees in Indianapolis." *Indiana Magazine of History* 102 (June 2006): 89–116.

Dora, Bob. "Along the Wabash: Dora Family History Leads Back to Indiana's Earliest Recorded European Settlers." *The Hoosier Genealogist: Connections* 50, no. 2 (Fall/Winter 2010): 68–79.

Folsom, Burton W., Jr. "John Jacob Astor and the Fur Trade: Testing the Role of Government; How an Entrepreneur Provided Better Products at Lower Cost." *The Freeman: Ideas on Liberty* 47, no. 6 (June 1997). http://www.thefreemanonline.org/featured/john-jacob-astor-and-the-fur-trade-testing-the-role-of-government/.

"In Search of Belonging: The Hispanic Religious Presence in Indianapolis." *Religion & Community*, 4, no. 1 (Fall 1998). http://www.polis.iupui.edu/RUC/Newsletters/Religion/vol4no1.htm.

Hickey, Gail M. "Asian Indians in Indiana." *Indiana Magazine of History* 102 (June 2006): 117–40.

Littlepage, Laura. "Latino Population Boom Impacts Indianapolis." In *Central Indiana*. January 2006. Center for Urban Policy and the Environment, Indiana University School of Public and Environmental Affairs, Indiana University–Purdue University, Indianapolis. http://www.policyinstitute.iu.edu/PubsPDFs/157_06-C01.pdf.

Marsh, Tanya D. "Following the Bee Line: History of the Jacob and Katherine Sherman Family Sheds Light on the Brightwood Neighborhood of Indianapolis." *The Hoosier Genealogist: Connections* 50, no. 1 (Spring/Summer 2010): 6–13.

McDonald, Earl E. "The Negro in Indiana before 1881." *Indiana Magazine of History* 27 (December 1931): 291–306.

Model, Suzanne. "The Economic Progress of European and East Asian Americans." *Annual Review of Sociology* 14 (1988): 363–80.

Moss, Richard. "Creating a Jewish American Identity in Indianapolis: The Jewish Welfare Federation and the Regulation of Leisure, 1920–1934." *Indiana Magazine of History* 103, (March 2007): 39–65.

Rose, Gregory S. "The Distribution of Indiana's Ethnic and Racial Minorities in 1850." *Indiana Magazine of History* 87 (September 1991): 225–60.

———. "Hoosier Origins: The Nativity of Indiana's United States-Born Population in 1850." *Indiana Magazine of History* 81 (September 1985): 201–32.

———. "Upland Southerners: The County Origins of Southern Migrants to Indiana by 1850." *Indiana Magazine of History* 82 (September 1986): 242–63.

Sample, Bradford. "A Truly Midwestern City: Indianapolis on the Eve of the Great Depression." *Indiana Magazine of History* 97 (June 2001): 129–47.

Wissing, Douglas. "Cook Good, Serve Generously, Price Modestly: The Shapiro's Story." *Traces of Indiana and Midwestern History* 21, no. 4 (Fall 2009): 4–15.

Index